Parliamentary Oversight Tools

This book investigates parliaments' capacity to oversee government activities, policies and expenditures. Utilising a comparative approach, the book presents a new examination of oversight tools and discusses the conditions under which such tools are employed effectively.

The result of a nine-year collaboration between the authors, this book draws from the findings of survey data collected by the World Bank Institute and the Inter-Parliamentary Union, analysing information from 120 parliaments. The book represents a rigorous attempt to test whether international organisations are correct in claiming that the quality of democracy and good governance can be improved by strengthening the oversight capacity of legislatures. It discusses the tools available to parliaments worldwide, and taking a comparative approach considers which tools are more or less common, how oversight capacity can be estimated, how oversight capacity is related to other institutional and constitutional factors, and above all what ensures that oversight tools are used effectively. This analysis reveals that while the quality of democracy and good governance benefits from effective oversight, oversight effectiveness cannot be reduced to oversight capacity. The book urges policy makers and reformers to change their approach from strengthening capacity to securing that the capacity is put to good use.

Parliamentary Oversight Tools will be of interest to students, scholars and practitioners of legislative politics and governance.

Riccardo Pelizzo is a parliamentary consultant and research advisor to the World Bank Institute.

Frederick Stapenhurst is a parliamentary consultant and research advisor to the World Bank Institute.

Routledge Research in Comparative Politics

Parliamentary Oversight Tools
A comparative analysis

Riccardo Pelizzo and
Frederick Stapenhurst

LONDON AND NEW YORK

First published 2012
by Routledge
2 Park Square, Milton Park, Abingdon, Oxon, OX14 4RN

Simultaneously published in the USA and Canada
by Routledge
711 Third Avenue, New York, NY10017

*Routledge is an imprint of the Taylor & Francis Group, an informa
business*

British Library Cataloguing in Publication Data
A catalogue record for this book is available from the British Library

Library of Congress Cataloging-in-Publication Data
Pelizzo, Riccardo.
Parliamentary oversight tools : a comparative analysis / Riccardo
Pelizzo and Frederick Stapenhurst.
p. cm. - - (Routledge research in comparative politics ; 45)
Includes bibliographical references and index.
1. Legislative oversight. 2. Executive-legislative relations.
3. Government accountability. 4. Political corruption- -Prevention.
5. Comparative government. I. Stapenhurst, Frederick. II. Title.
JF229.P36 2012
328.3'45- -dc23
2011024004

ISBN13: 978-0-415-61571-6 (hbk)
ISBN13: 978-0-203-15122-8 (ebk)

Typeset in Sabon
by Integra Software Services Pvt. Ltd, Pondicherry, India

Contents

List of illustrations

Diagrams

Figures

Tables

1 Introduction

The relatively recent surge in interest in the study of legislative over-sight and oversight tools reflects to a large extent a paradigm shift[1] in the international community.

In the 1960s it was largely believed that democracy and develop-ment went hand in hand. In the wake of the publication of Lipset's seminal work (1959), it was believed that development was good for democracy either because it created the conditions for a transition to democracy or because it created the conditions for the consolidation and the survival of democracy or all of the above.[2]

This conclusion, that was due to the insight of Lipset (1959), was based on an empirical finding that Lipset had discussed in his work, where he showed that the number of developed countries that were also democratic greatly outnumbered the number of countries that were developed and undemocratic. Lipset explained this finding by saying that socio-economic development is a necessary social requisite for the consolidation of democracy because "the more well-to-do a nation, the greater the chances that it will sustain democracy" (1959: 75).

According to Lispet there are several reasons why development is important for the stability, the consolidation and the survival of democracy. Development creates the conditions for the pluralisation of society which, in its turn, creates the condition for "the activation of more political actors" (O'Donnell, 1973: 71) as "political plur-alization is the political expression of social differentiation" (O'Donnell, 1973: 72). Development contributes to the consolidation and/or the survival of democratic regimes in a second respect. As a society develops, the middle class expands and middle classes generally hold pro-democratic attitudes (Lipset, 1960: 51). Development promotes democratic consolidation by making society more literate, more cultured, more exposed to democratic ideals, ideas and values. In this respect, Lipset (1960: 46, 50) noted that there is an inverse relationship between the electoral strength of extreme political groups and national income. In other words, voters and citizens of developed societies are less likely to support political groups whose aim is to overthrow the system from which the citizens benefit. And there is one more argument, though it was not developed by Lipset, for which economic development can create the conditions for the consolidation of democracy. As societies become more developed they have greater resources that they can redistribute among various groups to provide them with material incentives to coexist peacefully.

A very large body of research, sparked by the publication of Lipset (1959), has debated whether development is the single most important determinant of democratic consolidation.[3] For example, some of Lipset's critics have lamented that in Lipset's work it is not clear what is the arrow of causality. In other words, it is not clear whether democracy is a cause or a consequence of development. In this respect Macridis (1968: 86) noted that "at the end of this excellent study (*Political Man*), the reader is not sure whether open democracies are affluent because they are open and democratic or whether it is the other way round". Much in the same vein, Rustow (1968: 48) observed that:

> correlations between contemporary social, economic and political indicators for series of countries give no clue whatsoever as to the direction, if any, of causality. If authors such as Lipset (1959, 1960) or Cutright (1965) find democracy highly correlated with education, affluence and urbanization ... we still do not know (1) whether college graduates, rich people and urban dwellers make better democrats or (2) whether democracy is a system of government that encourages schooling, wealth and urban residence or (3) whether both democracy and its alleged correlates result from further unexplored causes.

More recently, Weiner (1987: 861) critically remarked that "the relationship between rates of growth (or rates of social mobilization), class structure, and the development and the persistence of democratic institutions in low-income countries has had several variant contradictory hypotheses".[4]

The most cogent criticism of Lipset's theory and, more broadly, of modernisation theory was proposed by Huntington (1968) who asserted that democracy was not a value in and by itself, that democracy might not be conducive to socio-economic development and that socio-economic development in turn could actually destabilise recently established democracies. Huntington's notions largely shaped the thinking of the international community on democracy. International organisations and bilateral donors generally focused on the promotion of socio-economic development and on economic and technical issues, and typically refrained from addressing governance issues – such as democracy and corruption – that were believed to be "political" in nature and hence either outside their terms of reference, as was the case in the World Bank, or sensitive issues generally to be avoided.

The 1990s witnessed two major transformations that resulted in the paradigm change. In the early 1990s, with the collapse of the Soviet Union and its satellite states, the end of the Cold War and the bipolar order, the considerations that had led international relations scholars, such as Huntington, to underline the shortcomings of democratic rule in modernising societies, vanished. Indeed, Huntington (1991) himself made it clear that his old concerns no longer applied and that democracy should be regarded as a "good thing" and international organisations (most notably the European Bank for Reconstruction and Development) were set up with the express purpose of facilitating transitions to democracy and/or of consolidating democracy where it had recently been established.

The other change that created the conditions for a paradigm change was that a series of new studies on the determinants of sustainable economic growth and socio-economic development, illustrated that development was not simply an economic or technical issue, but also a "political" issue (e.g. Kaufman, 1997; Kaufman *et al.*, 2006; Rose-Ackermann, 1978, 1999). Specifically, a new wave of developmental studies made it clear that political problems or pathologies, such as corruption, were detrimental to socio-economic development. These studies suggested that the promotion of good governance through political development and institutionalisation were essential for the success of socio-economic development more generally.

Attempts to promote democracy have tried to do so by either promoting political development directly, or more obliquely by promoting socio-economic development but with a focus on "participation" and "social accountability". Generally, the organisations devoted to the promotion of one type of development are not involved in the promotion of the other (Carothers, 2009). Nevertheless, both sets of organisations recognise the importance of legislatures. A cursory look at the publications produced by the World Bank is indicative of the paradigm change noted above: legislatures were credited with the ability to improve the quality of democracy by holding governments to account (Stapenhurst, Pelizzo, von Trapp and Olson, 2008), to prevent corruption (Stapenhurst, Johnston and Pelizzo, 2006), to reduce poverty (Stapenhurst and Pelizzo, 2002), to rebuild post-conflict societies (O'Brien, Stapenhurst and Johnston, 2008) and to improve public finance (Wehner, 2004).

And in so far as legislatures' ability to create the conditions to achieve all these policy-relevant objectives is a function of their institutional capacity to oversee the executive, international organisations became interested in assessing, measuring and quantifying the institutional capacity, the formal powers, the activities performed and the effectiveness of legislatures.[5] One of the first such efforts was a survey conducted jointly by the World Bank Institute (WBI) and the Inter-Parliamentary Union (IPU) in 2001, which focused on executive–legislative relationships and on the oversight tools that legislatures have developed to oversee the government, especially with regard to the budget process.

The first serious effort to estimate legislative oversight capacity was made in 2001 when the World Bank Institute (WBI) and the Inter-Parliamentary Union (IPU) conducted a survey of 83 legislatures to assess oversight capacity worldwide, that is, whether legislatures had a weak/strong capacity to oversee the executive, and to understand which factors were responsible for variance in such capacity. A number of studies were carried out examining the relationship between legislative oversight and the form of government, the level of development, the quality of democracy and the level of corruption (e.g. Pelizzo and Stapenhurst, 2004; Pelizzo and Stapenhurst, 2008, Yamamoto, 2008).

The principal findings of these and similar studies were that all legislatures have at least some oversight capacity; that legislatures operating in parliamentary systems are, on average, better equipped (in terms of oversight tools) than legislatures in semi-presidential or presidential systems to oversee the government; and that oversight capacity, measured in terms of the number of oversight tools is not simply a function of the form of government (that is, parliamentary, semi-presidential or presidential), but is related to other conditions such as a country's level of socio-economic development and level of democracy. Some of the studies argued that legislatures' greater oversight capacity was not simply associated with higher levels of democratic quality, but that it was actually responsible for the higher democratic quality and made oversight tools available to the legislature (Pelizzo and Stapenhurst, 2008). Finally, with regard to the oversight of the budget, some studies indicated that legislatures in semi-presidential systems were the least involved in the preparation and examination of the budget, but were the most active in using ex-post audit reports as a tool to oversee budget implementation and that while they were not as involved as legislatures in presidential systems in the confirmation and approval of the budget, they were certainly more so than legislatures in parliamentary systems.

These findings were of some importance for three reasons. The first was that they shed some light on phenomena and relationships (between variables) that had never been subjected to rigorous analysis, for the lack of quantitative data. The second reason was that these analyses, in addition to identifying strong correlations between the variables of interest (oversight capacity, form of government, quality of democracy and level of corruption) hypothesised clear causal relations between these variables. Specifically, these studies hypothesised that the lower levels of corruption recorded in countries where the legislature is better equipped to perform its oversight tasks were due to the fact that oversight capacity, for a variety of reasons that will be discussed later at greater length, is instrumental in curbing corruption. Hence, on the basis of this evidence, these studies suggested that no successful effort to prevent or curb corruption could be made without strengthening the oversight capacity of legislatures. The third reason was that by formulating hypotheses that could not be adequately tested with available data it called for a new survey to be conducted among legislatures around the world. Such a (second) survey was conducted by WBI and IPU in 2009.

Our objective in this book is twofold. The first objective is to investigate how legislative oversight has evolved over the period 2001 to 2009 and to re-examine legislatures' capacity to oversee government activities and policies. Importantly, we distinguish between oversight *capacity* and oversight *effectiveness*. By analysing the more recent survey data collected from 120 legislatures, we show what oversight tools are available to legislatures worldwide, which tools are most widely used, how both oversight capacity and oversight effectiveness can be estimated and how such capacity and effectiveness is related to other institutional and constitutional factors such as form of government, quality of democracy and level of corruption.

For the past 15 years, international organisations, such as the World Bank and the United Nations Development Program, along with bilateral aid agencies such as the United Kingdom's Department for International Development and Canada's International Development Agency and non-governmental organisations like the National Democratic Institute and the Parliamentary Centre, devoted resources to consolidation of democracy in newly established democratic regimes and/or the promotion of good governance. In addition to discussing the conditions under which oversight capacity and effectiveness is greater, we perform some analyses to assess the policy implications of oversight capacity and effectiveness. Specifically we look at the impact of oversight capacity and effectiveness on the quality of democracy and on the level of corruption. Scholars such as Fish (2006) and Burnell (2009) have noted that the strengthening of legislatures is an essential element of any serious effort to promote democracy and/or good governance. Strong legislatures are believed to be better equipped to oversee government activities, debate government bills, assess government policies, monitor policy implementation, prevent misallocation of resources, and by doing so, to improve governance, prevent corruption, create the conditions for socio-economic growth and be instrumental in reducing poverty (Stapenhurst and Pelizzo, 2002).

If the first generation of studies looking at legislative oversight worldwide made use of the 2001 WBI-IPU database, this book represents the first comprehensive study of what could be called a second generation of studies, based on the 2009 data. In this book we attempt to map legislative oversight capacity globally and to assess how it has evolved since 2001. We examine how such capacity varies across levels of development, forms of government and across legislatures. Furthermore, in addition to presenting some information as to which tools parliaments can employ to oversee government activity and to keep governments accountable, we present a more comprehensive analysis of the oversight tools that legislatures employ to regulate and control the behaviour of governments. We also assess whether the quality of democracy and levels of good governance are affected by legislatures' ability to control governments.

For the first time, we distinguish between legislative oversight *capacity* and legislative oversight *effectiveness*. We undertake statistical analyses of both, and find that international organisations and bilateral donors alike have focused too much on the former and not enough on the latter. In other words, international organisations and bilateral agencies – and legislatures themselves – need to focus not on simply adopting more oversight tools, but rather on making legislatures use their oversight tools effectively.

The second, and possibly more ambitious, objective of this book is to develop, present and test a strategic interaction model to explain why under some circumstances oversight tools are used effectively and under other circumstances they are either not used effectively or, worse, they are not used at all. In a nutshell, our strategic interaction model posits that whether oversight tools are adopted and used effectively or not depends on whether there is a popular demand for good governance and effective oversight and on how the ruling class responds to popular demands.

This book is arranged as follows:

In Chapter 2, we first note that scholars have proposed different definitions for oversight. Some, such as Ogul (1976) and Maffio (2002), noted that it is not just supervision of what the executive branch of government has done, but also supervision of the executive's legislative proposals. By contrast, Olson and Mezey (1991) and McCubbins and Schwartz (1984) suggest that oversight refers to the set of activities that a parliament performs to evaluate the implementation of policies.[6] Others, such as Doering (1995), Drewry (1989), Blondel (1973) and Olson (2008) distinguish between oversight and scrutiny.[7] The National Democratic Institute (NDI) (2000: 19) defined oversight as "the obvious follow-on activity linked to law-making. After participating in law-making, the legislature's main role is to see whether laws are effectively implemented and whether, in fact, they address and correct the problems, as intended by their drafters." This definition captures the role that legislatures play in overseeing government policies ex-post, but overlooks the role that legislatures may play before a policy is enacted. In this book we use the ex-post definition, since we are mostly concerned with the role of the legislature in tracking and overseeing public expenditures; that is, in policy *implementation*, rather than in policy formulation more generally. We also consider why oversight is important when one examines the accountability of governments to their electorates and how legislative oversight tools are used to reinforce different accountability relationships.

In Chapter 3, we perform a comprehensive review of legislative oversight tools. Ogul (1976) suggested seven "opportunity factors" that promote or limit the potential for oversight in the United States. These are: legal authority or obligation, adequate staff, importance of the policy being overseen, the legislative committee system and its status within the legislature, the scope of oversight given executive-legislative relations, political party influences and the priorities of individual legislators. Olson and Mezey (1991), Norton and Ahmed (1999) and Crowther and Olson (2002), among others, go further, distinguishing between internal factors that influence oversight and external or contextual factors. Wang (2005) usefully proposed a diagrammatic framework for studying these variables, which we modify to take into account additional oversight tools. We go on to consider *external* oversight tools – supreme audit institutions (SAIs), ombuds offices and anti-corruption agencies. Then, we review *internal* oversight tools, namely, committees and special commissions of inquiry, confirmation of appointments, no confidence, censure and impeachment, questions and interpellations and debates in plenary.

Furthermore, we analyse the use of legislative oversight tools in the lower legislative chambers – the institutions within legislatures that are most typically charged with government oversight. In this chapter, in addition to summarising the main results of the 2001 survey, we present the evidence generated by the 2009 survey. In doing so, we show what are the oversight tools that legislatures can use to oversee government activity and how these tools are distributed across countries, levels of development and forms of government. Particular attention is paid to whether the results of this new survey are consistent with, and therefore corroborate, the findings generated by the 2001 survey. Specific attention is paid to three sets of issues that were extensively discussed following the earlier survey, namely, the distribution of oversight tools in countries with different forms of government (that is, parliamentary, semi-presidential and presidential) together with the institutional correlates of this distribution. The analysis of the 2009 survey data reveals, consistent with what has already been argued in the literature, three sets of findings, namely: (i) that all legislatures have at least one oversight tool and usually more than one; (ii) that some oversight tools are more common than others; and (iii) that the distribution of tools in 2009 is very consistent with that recorded in 2001. For the first time, we compare the oversight capacity in lower and upper chambers. By doing so we highlight some of the similarities and the differences in the oversight tools of upper chambers.

In Chapter 4, we turn to the second of our main empirical questions – the relationship between legislative oversight and the quality of democracy. We show that by applying Morlino's (2005) framework to the analysis of the quality of democracy, *effective* oversight is a significant determinant of the quality of democracy; we also demonstrate that oversight *capacity* is not a significant determinant. Morlino suggested that any successful effort of measuring democracy should take into consideration the fact that democracy is a multi-dimensional phenomenon and that the notion of democratic quality could be used to refer to (i) the procedures employed by the democratic regime; (ii) the output of the democratic regime; and (iii) the outcome of the democratic regime, that is, whether it is stable and legitimate. Each of these macro-dimensions, he argued, entails several sub-dimensions. For example, the quality of democracy in terms of outcome can easily be assessed on the basis of whether a democratic regime is responsive to the citizens, whether it is perceived to be responsive or on whether it is regarded as a legitimate one; the quality of democracy in terms of outputs can be assessed on whether and how well the democratic regime is able to promote socio-economic (as well as political) equality and to protect individual rights freedoms; while the quality of democracy in terms of procedures can be assessed on the basis of several sub-dimensions, such as the rule of law, participation, competition, electoral accountability and inter-institutional accountability. Inter-institutional accountability refers to the legislature's (and to the judiciary's) ability to oversee the activities of the executive branch. And in so far as a legislature's ability to oversee the executive branch is facilitated by the range of oversight tools at its disposal, it is reasonable to hypothesise that legislatures which have more oversight tools at their disposal have a greater oversight capacity and that this greater oversight capacity is conducive to greater inter-institutional accountability and, ultimately, to a democracy of a higher quality.

In this chapter we test whether and to what extent the quality of democracy increases along with legislatures' oversight capacity and effectiveness. The results of our empirical analyses reveal that while the quality of democracy is related to the effectiveness of oversight and to the fact that a country is democratic (at least formally if not substantively), oversight capacity is not as important as previous studies (Pelizzo, 2008) had suggested. Furthermore, our analyses also reveal that, contrary to what international organisations and bilateral agencies had initially believed (USAID, 2000), effectiveness of oversight is not a function of oversight capacity. We conclude by arguing that this evidence should induce international organisations and bilateral agencies to modify their democracy and development promotion strategies. What they need to promote is effective oversight, not simply oversight capacity.

In Chapter 5, we examine how the international community came to conceptualise corruption and how they – and others – have focused on increasing legislative oversight capacity as part of a broader, multi-stakeholder strategy to decrease corruption. Specifically we show that as international organisations came to realise that corruption could be detrimental to socio-economic development and poverty reduction, they started to regard the reduction of corruption as a key element of their development promotion strategies. Furthermore, corruption came to be regarded as a multi-faceted phenomenon that could only be addressed by developing equally multi-faceted anti-corruption strategies, a key component of which was the strengthening of legislatures' oversight capacity. In other words, international organisations reached the conclusion that legislatures' oversight potential or capacity was essential for ensuring effective oversight, which in turn was regarded as one of the effective ways to minimise corruption. We point out that this relationship was generally assumed, and was not subjected to rigorous empirical scrutiny – and in this chapter we subject some of the causal claims advanced by international organisations to empirical verification. In particular, we highlight the relationship between development and corruption; corruption and the *effectiveness* of oversight; oversight *effectiveness* and oversight *capacity*; and oversight *capacity* and corruption.

In Chapter 6, we show that while the existence of legislative oversight tools matters in that such tools improve the quality of governance and the legitimacy of the political systems. Their impact is conditional and it depends on the presence of contextual factors. We present a case study of the Parliament of Ghana and show two substantive results: first that as the Parliament of Ghana has become a more pro-active overseer of the executive, the functioning of the political system has improved and the legitimacy of the political system has increased; second that the success of the Ghanaian Parliament was made possible by the effective use of oversight tools at its disposal and a set of specific contextual factors.

In Chapter 7, we present our strategic interaction model. This chapter represents a major point of departure from previous scholarship on oversight tools, oversight capacity, oversight activity and effectiveness. Previous studies generally over-emphasised the importance of macro-level factors such as institutional design, constitutional dispositions, normative dispositions and cultural predispositions to explain why oversight is performed effectively and may contribute to improving both the quality of democracy and/or the level of good governance. The problem of each of these macro-level explanations is that they, for the most part, are static, neglect the role of agential factors, view agency as a simple consequence of structural conditions and, above all, cannot explain a very simple question, that is, Why do some legislatures decide to use effectively the oversight tools at their disposal and take a good look at what the executive does and some others decide to do otherwise? Legislature's decision to act cannot be accounted for simply in structural terms. The explanation has to be behavioural in nature. It has to address why a certain type of behaviour is triggered in one instance and it is not triggered in another. The answer to this question, we argue in Chapter 7, has to be found in the strategic interaction between political actors, namely the ruling class on the one hand and the civil society on the other hand. Specifically, in Chapter 7 we suggest that voter demands play a key role in shaping the set of incentives confronting political actors, as well as their strategies and choices. We claim that it is precisely the interplay between voter demands and politicians' strategic considerations that explains why oversight capacity is or is not used effectively.

In Chapter 8, we go on to test our strategic interaction model by analysing the performance of Public Accounts Committees (PACs). In doing so, after presenting the major explanations of what makes PACs work well, after discussing the data sources used in previous studies, after critically assessing the explanatory merit of the PAC literature, we go on to test how well our strategic interaction model works in explaining the effective functioning of PACs. We believe that this chapter is of importance not only because it introduces a new focus in the analysis of legislative oversight and the activity of PACs but also because it provides the international community with a compelling case for reconsidering and reshaping some of its legislative strengthening strategies.

Building on this discussion we draw two sets of conclusions. The first set concerns the direction that the comparative study of oversight should take in the future, to shed some light on the areas and questions that the data currently available prevent us from adequately addressing. The second set of conclusions concerns how the international community may want to rethink some of its assumptions regarding legislative oversight and legislative strengthening. While the international community, international organisations and practitioners have so far believed that the strengthening of legislatures' oversight capacity is in and by itself a solution for all kinds of problems, as strong oversight capacity can make governments work better, that it can improve the quality of democracy, that may reduce and possibly eliminate corruption, we suggest instead that what legislatures need effectively to oversee in government activities is not greater oversight capacity but the willingness to use the oversight tools at their disposal. The main conclusion of this study, for practitioners and international organisations alike, is that their task now is not just that of inducing a ruling class, that may have various reasons to preserve the status quo, to introduce institutional change but also that of inducing the ruling class to secure the effective functioning of the newly created institutions. For instance, now that some countries that have traditionally had low levels of good governance (and high levels of corruption) have adopted PACs in their effort to keep their government more accountable and make their political systems work better, they must ensure that PACs perform the tasks for which they were established. In this book, we suggest that one way to do so is to create and sustain, through a proper media campaign, a popular demand. In the absence of such demand, reforms are either not made or they are not adequately implemented.

We present our conclusions in Chapter 9. We recap the claims we have formulated through this book, noting that agency theory has been a missing element in the study of legislative oversight heretofore. We explore the implications of our findings for scholars and practitioners alike; and we stress the importance of a free media in the promotion of democratic development and good governance. We end with three lessons that can be learned from our research: that international organisations need to learn to learn, consider the importance of agency as well as structural/institutional factors when strengthening legislatures and to focus on the critical element of popular demand in the promotion of reforms.

2 Theoretical foundations of legislative oversight

Introduction

In this chapter, we present the theoretical foundations of legislative oversight, focusing on principal-agent theory and on institutional approaches. Specific attention is paid to how these theories relate to legislative oversight. However, there is no consensus among scholars on the definition of legislative oversight (Olson, 2008) and, like the broader field of legislative studies, the concept is under-theorised. We thus lay the groundwork for our theoretical model of legislative oversight, which we present in Chapter 7.

There are few global analyses.[1] Most analyses are undertaken at a country or regional level, often within a loose theoretical framework (e.g., Olson and Norton, 1996; Norton and Ahmed, 1999). These studies typically examine legislative functions within countries more generally, and do not focus solely, or particularly, on oversight. Furthermore, while there is a plethora of studies on the oversight function in the United States, there is only a relatively small number of studies outside the United States.

Scholars have proposed different definitions for oversight. Schick (1976) noted that it consists of legislative supervision of the policies and programs enacted by government. Others, such as Ogul (1976) and Maffio (2002), noted that it is not just supervision of what the executive branch of government has done, but also supervision of the executive's legislative proposals. By contrast, Olson and Mezey (1991) and McCubbins and Schwartz (1984) suggest that oversight refers to the set of activities that a parliament performs to evaluate the implementation of policies.[2] Some scholars, such as Doering (1995), Drewry (1989), Blondel (1973) and Olson (2008) distinguish between oversight and scrutiny.[3]

The National Democratic Institute (NDI) (2000: 19) defined oversight as "the obvious follow-on activity linked to law-making. After participating in law-making, the legislature's main role is to see whether laws are effectively implemented and whether, in fact, they address and correct the problems, as intended by their drafters." This definition captures the role that legislatures play in overseeing government policies ex-post, but overlooks the role that legislatures may play before a policy is enacted. The NDI definition is implicit in Olson's (2008) distinction between oversight (which is similar to this definition) and "scrutiny", which concerns the role of the legislature in preparing policies. In this book we use the ex-post definition, since we are mostly concerned with the role of the legislature in tracking and overseeing public expenditures; that is, in policy *implementation*, rather than in policy formulation more generally.

Within the context of ex-ante and ex-post oversight in the United States, Ogul (1976) suggested seven "opportunity factors" that promote or limit the potential for oversight. These are: legal authority or obligation, adequate staff, importance of the policy being overseen, the legislative committee system and its status within the legislature, the scope of oversight given executive–legislative relations, political party influences and the priorities of individual legislators. Olson and Mezey (1991), Olson and Norton (1996), Norton and Ahmed (1999) and Crowther and Olson (2002) go further, distinguishing between internal factors that influence oversight and external or contextual factors. We return to this distinction in Chapter 3.

This chapter is organised as follows: first, we consider the theoretical foundations of legislative oversight. Then we consider agency theory and show how principal-agent theory can be used to examine government accountability and which oversight tools are used to reinforce the accountability relationships which exist between government, the legislature and citizens. In the third section, we turn to the institutional theories of path dependency, archetypes, isomorphism and convergence. We then examine the role of legislative oversight tools in the promotion of both vertical, horizontal and diagonal accountability. The final section presents conclusions.

Section one: theoretical foundations

The *theories* that guide our research are drawn from the literature on corruption, accountability, and legislative oversight from the institutionalist school of thought, especially the rational choice, historical and sociological sub-schools. The nexus between these theories is not well developed, and one of our objectives is to synthesise these theories with regard to the oversight function of legislatures.

The methodological approach we follow is *neo-institutionalist*. We reject both the pure *classical institutionalist* and pure *behaviouralist* approaches. The pure *classical institutional* approach was rooted in law and legal institutions and focused " ... on how the 'rules' channeled behavior ... [and] ... on how and why the rules came into being in the first place, and, above all, whether or not the rules worked on behalf of the common good" (Rhodes, Binder and Rockman, 2006: xii). This approach is largely descriptive and atheoretical and fails to provide a framework for our analyses.

The pure *behaviouralist* approach was a reaction against the classical institutional approach and was grounded in the recognition that "[p]eople frequently did not adhere to the rules, and [that] informal groups of peers often became more influential than the formal organizational settings these individuals found themselves in" (Rhodes, Binder and Rockman, 2006: xii). This approach does not provide a useful framework for our analysis, as it does not consider institutional factors that shape and influence behaviour.

The *neo-institutionalist* approach emerged as a reaction to the pure behaviouralist approach and comprises elements of both pure approaches. It connotes " ... a set of theoretical ideas and hypotheses concerning the relations between institutional characteristics and political agency, performance and change" (March and Olsen, 2006: 4). The neo-institutionalist approach offers a better conceptual framework than the earlier behavioural approach, which generally assumed that "[i]nstitutions were ... empty shells to be filled by individual roles, statuses and values ... [and that o]nce you had these individual-level properties, and summed them up properly, there was no need to study institutions; they were epiphenomenal" (Shepsle, 1989: 113).

However, there is no consensus in the literature regarding the exact meaning of *neo-institutionalism*. According to Scott (2001: 33), there are " ... two quite distinct groups: the *historical* and the *rational choice* theorists." In this regard, Scott is implicitly supported by North (1990), Thelen and Steinmo (1992), and Sanders (2006). However, Hall and Taylor (1996) add a third school, that of *sociological* institutionalism. All three variants of this school are outlined below.

Historical institutionalists define institutions as the formal or informal procedures, routines, norms and conventions embedded in the organisational structure of the polity (Hall and Taylor, 1996). By contrast, *rational choice* scholars believe that institutions are important mainly as features of a strategic context, imposing constraints on self-interested behaviour. Historical institutionalists and rational choice practitioners largely agree that " ... institutions constitute the humanly devised constraints that shape human interaction" (North, 1990: 384); however, they differ in the object and time-span of their studies. Rational choice advocates tend to be more interested in the "microcosmic game"; that is,

> ... the particular interaction of preference-holding, utility-seeking individuals within a set of (stable) institutional constraints ... [while] historical institutionalists are more concerned with the construction, maintenance and adaptation of institutions and are ... generally more concerned with the long-term evolution and outcome of a welter of interactions among goal-seeking actors, both within institutions, and their challengers outside.
>
> (Sanders, 2006: 42).

Despite these differences, "[t]here is no reason why the two approaches should be viewed as antithetical ... They may well be complementary" (Sanders, 2006: 43). Hall and Taylor (1996) note that *sociological institutionalists* focus on the processes whereby institutions "borrow" from the existing world of institutional templates. In other words, sociological institutionalists emphasise the way in which the existing institutional world circumscribes the range of institutional creation. In short, rational choice scholars are increasingly aware that actors are constrained by structures, while the sociological institutionalists now recognise that structure without agency cannot fully explain outcomes, such as reduced corruption. In this book, we draw on all three institutionalist schools. As a result, the methodological approach adopted in this book can be regarded as *neo-institutionalist*. In adopting this approach, we acknowledge that institutionalism has " ... experienced a sort of *renaissance* among political scientists" (Pelizzo *et al.*, 2006: 775), and that neo-institutionalismhas moved beyond the simple belief that institutions matter, to an understanding of "whether, why and how much they matter". In following this approach, we examine whether, why and how much legislative oversight contributes to the control of corruption and how much it is related to the quality of democracy.

In an attempt to cut through the complexity and confusion surrounding the concept of government accountability, we utilise the *principal-agent* theory drawn from the rational choice school of institutionalism. We do so because it provides both a theoretical framework and starting point for the analyses in the remainder of this book and a cornerstone of our theoretical model, which we present in Chapter 7.

Section two: principal-agent theory

The principal-agent theory emphasises the institutional mechanisms whereby *principals* can monitor and enforce compliance on their *agents*. This theory is particularly appropriate for explaining the accountability relationship between citizens (as principals) and the executive and the legislature (both as agents) on the one hand, and between the legislature (acting as principal, on behalf of citizens) and both the executive and the bureaucracy on the other hand.[4]

Diagram 2.1 applies the principal-agent theory to legislative oversight. The ultimate principals are citizens; the ultimate agents are

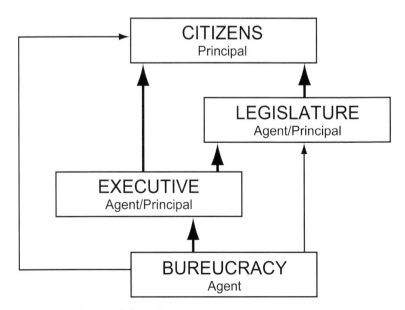

Diagram 2.1 Accountability relations as agency

civil servants (the bureaucracy). The executive and the legislature are both principals and agents. The executive, as agent, is accountable directly to citizens through the electoral process, and to the legislature which acts on behalf of citizens and exercises an oversight function over the executive.[5]

Fukuyama (2004a), referencing Berle and Means (1932), notes that ownership has been divorced from management in private sector corporations and that managers (or "agents") have subsequently been charged with looking after the interests of the owners (or "principals"). A problem arises in that " ... agents often face individual incentives that differ sharply from those of the principals". This time referencing Jensen and Meckling (1976), Fukuyama (2004b) also highlights the "agency costs" which principals incur to ensure that agents do their bidding; for example, monitoring agent behaviour.

Rose-Ackerman (1978), Weingast and Moran (1983), and Moe (1984) adapted the principal-agent framework to explain public behaviour. According to Fukuyama (2004a: 190–91),

> [I]n the public sector, the principals are the public at large. In a democracy, their first level agents are their elected representatives; the legislators act as principals with regard to executive branch agents delegated to carry out the policies that they have legislated. [Problems occur] when individual agents – government officials – put their own pecuniary interests ahead of their principals.

To counteract such behaviour, and to better align principal-agent interests, " ... greater transparency in the activity of agents is required, coupled with the holding of agents accountable for their actions through a variety of rewards and punishments".[6]

Fukuyama (2004b) identifies three problems that arise in applying the principal-agent model to public sector governance. First, the goals of public sector organisations are often unclear. Agents can only carry out the will of the principals if the principals are clear in what they want the agents to do. Second, formal systems of monitoring and accountability either entail very high transaction costs or lack the specificity of the underlying activity. And third, the appropriate degree of delegated discretion will vary over time. All delegation involves a tradeoff between efficiency and risk – and the appropriate level may be difficult to determine, and vary from one setting to another.[7]

Criticisms of the principal-agent theory seem to apply as much to legislative–executive relations as they do in a more general sense. First, citizens are often not clear about what they would like their agents (the executive and the legislature) to do, leaving substantial room for agents to develop their own, self-serving, goals. The transaction costs for citizens to oversee executive government or the bureaucracy may be too high – resulting in a "derived" oversight function of the legislature to hold the government and the bureaucracy to account. There is substantial information asymmetry. The bureaucracy (as agent) has more detailed knowledge than the executive, the legislature or citizens (as principals). The executive (as agent) has more information than citizens or the legislature (as principals). And the legislature (as agent) has more information than citizens (as principal).

However, these criticisms do not negate the principal-agent relationship in legislative–executive relations. Instead, these weaknesses have stimulated the development of specific tools and mechanisms (e.g. legislative oversight tools) that principals (i.e. the legislature) can use to hold agents (i.e. the executive and bureaucracy) to account.

Legislatures have developed oversight tools and mechanisms to help them, as principals, hold their agents (the executive and the bureaucracy) to account. The literature has not considered how the various oversight tools are used in these accountability relationships. We present this in Diagram 2.2. Considering external oversight tools first,

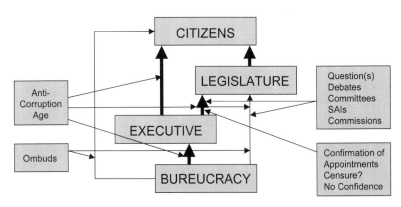

Diagram 2.2 Accountability relationships and oversight tools

supreme audit institutions (SAIs) are mostly used to improve legislative oversight over the bureaucracy, although they may also be used to enhance executive accountability to the legislature. By contrast, ombuds offices can be used directly by citizens to enforce bureaucratic accountability, although there is often a role for legislative follow-up. For example, in Finland the ombuds office reports to the legislature and there is an oversight committee to follow up on the ombuds' recommendations. Anti-corruption agencies can help enforce the accountability relations of both the executive and the bureaucracy; again, there is a direct legislative role where the agency reports to the legislature and especially to a legislative committee (as in the states of New South Wales, Queensland and Western Australia). Regarding internal oversight tools, committees/commissions, questions and interpellations, and debates are used to enforce bureaucratic and executive accountability to the legislature. Executive accountability to the legislature is enforced by reviewing appointments, censure and impeachment, and no confidence motions.

In short, oversight tools have been developed in response to agency problems – a point to which we will return, to a much greater extent, in Chapter 8. There is considerable power and information asymmetry between the executive (and the bureaucracy) and the legislature – and the legislatures have developed a set of tools and mechanisms to help them hold governments to account. One would expect that the more oversight tools available to a legislature, the greater legislative oversight and the less corruption.

However, the empirical analysis in Chapters 3–7 suggests that one needs to look beyond agency theory to explain variations in legislative oversight, and corruption, across countries. In a "pure" agency case, one could expect agents to be unconstrained by institutional structures. Empirical evidence shows that this is not the case – the freedom of agents to act is constrained by institutional context, rules and structures. But how does this relate to legislative oversight?

Given the empirical findings of Chapters 3–7, it is pertinent to consider why there is a difference between parliamentary, semi-presidential and presidential systems regarding the use of oversight tools and to what extent these differences might be explained through institutional concepts such as templates for organising/archetypical systems, path-dependency and isomorphism.

We now turn to such a consideration here.

Section three: institutional context

Recognising that " ... the beginning of wisdom in approaching institutional theory is to recognize that there is not one but several variants" (Scott, 1987: 493), we draw upon the notion of the impact of the institutional context and templates for organising/archetypical systems.

Institutional theory suggests that regularised organisational behaviours are the result of ideas, values and beliefs that have their origin in the institutional context (Meyer and Rowan, 1977; Meyer, Scott and Deal, 1983; Zucker, 1983). According to this notion, organisations have to accommodate institutional expectations in order to prosper and survive, even though these expectations may have little to do with technical notions of performance accomplishment (D'Aunno, Sutton, and Price, 1991; DiMaggio and Powell, 1991; Scott, 1987). Thus, for example, a legislature may be organised as a parliament, as opposed to a congress, not because that form of organisation has been analysed and found to be the most efficient and effective form, but rather because a parliament has been defined, *a priori*, as the most appropriate way of organising a legislature. In other words, institutional theory suggests that legislative organisational behaviours are responses to institutional pressures. DiMaggio and Powell (1991: 27) term these "institutional pressures" which lead organisations to adopt the same organisational form as "templates for organizing".

But if archetypical templates explain the initial adoption of legislative types, what explains their subsequent evolution? In the first instance, the notion of *path-dependency* is useful – the development of the type of government can be said to be "path-dependent"; that is, it will be mediated by the contextual features of a given situation, often inherited from the past, and not follow the same trajectory nor generate the same results everywhere. Path-dependency assumes that there will be long periods of institutional continuity, which will be interrupted only at "critical junctures" of radical change (March and Olsen, 2006: 12, drawing on Streek and Thelen, 2005). As a result, some institutional factors have changed considerably.

At the same time, there appears to be pressure for *convergence*. In Ghana, for example, there are plans to establish a parliamentary research office – a feature traditionally found in presidential systems. In many parliamentary countries, legislatures are establishing stronger committees and enhanced ex-ante budget oversight power. Again, these features are more commonly associated with legislatures in presidential countries. At the same time, legislatures in many non-Commonwealth countries, such as Liberia, Kosovo and Indonesia, are establishing Public Accounts Committees, a feature exclusive to Westminster-style parliamentary systems until just a few years ago (Hamilton and Stapenhurst, 2011). An explanation for this can be found in *mimetic isomorphism* – a term initially introduced by DiMaggio and Powell (1983) to explain the convergence of processes and structure of organisation through imitation. The logic behind this is the belief that certain institutional processes or structures are beneficial and therefore worthy of imitation.

In sum, one would expect path-dependency to explain why some contextual factors (e.g. form of government and type of electoral system) are similar across countries, reflecting the initial template for design. But over time, there is movement away from the template, and the notions of convergence and mimetic isomorphism can explain similarities in legislative oversight institutions, despite different organisational templates.

Section four: accountability and legislatures

The notion of accountability is an amorphous concept that is difficult to define in precise terms. However, broadly speaking, *accountability* exists in relationships where an individual or institution, and the tasks they perform, is subject to another's oversight, direction or request that they explain or justify their actions. Thus, the concept of accountability involves two distinct stages: *answerability* and *enforcement*. Answerability refers to the obligation of the accountee (for the purpose of this book, the government, its agencies and public officials) to provide information about its decisions and actions and to justify them to the public and those institutions of accountability tasked with providing oversight (for this book, the legislature). Enforcement suggests that the public or the institution responsible for accountability can sanction the offending party or remedy the contravening behaviour. As such, different institutions of accountability might be responsible for either or both of these stages.

The prevailing view of *horizontal accountability* is that it is the capacity of state institutions to check abuses by other public agencies and branches of government, or the requirement for agencies to

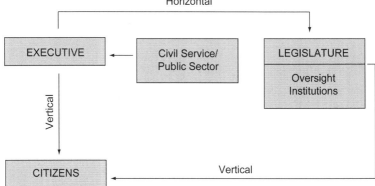

Diagram 2.3 Traditional concepts of accountability

report horizontally to other agencies. This concept has been examined by academics from the discipline of public administration. Conversely, the concept of *vertical accountability*, emanating from the political science and development disciplines, is the means through which citizens, mass media and civil society seek to enforce standards of good performance on officials (O'Donnell, 1999; Goetz and Gaventa, 2001; Cavill and Sohail, 2004). See Diagram 2.3. (By contrast, Bovens [2005a, 2005b, 2006] presents a differing conception of what constitutes vertical and horizontal accountability. He delineates between *horizontal* and *vertical accountability* based on the relationship between the agent and the entity demanding the accountability. If it is a principal-agent relationship [as in the legislature and the executive], it is a form of vertical accountability. If there is no hierarchal relationship, Bovens [2005a, 2005b, 2006] argues that it must be a form of horizontal accountability. Therefore, the lack of hierarchical relationship between civil society and public officials – that is, civil society cannot make enforceable demands on public officials – implies a *horizontal accountability* relationship.)

It is not our intention in this book to seek for a conceptual synthesis between these different conceptualisations of accountability (for that, we refer the reader to Stapenhurst, 2011). Rather, we will build upon the prevailing views of horizontal, vertical, diagonal and social accountability.

Newer concepts of accountability have emerged: social accountability and diagonal accountability. The former, defined as "society-driven horizontal accountability" seeks to provide direct

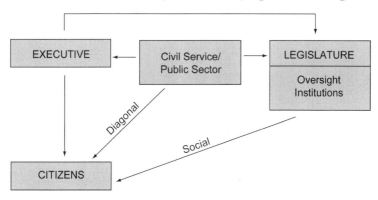

Diagram 2.4 Newer concepts of accountability

answerability from government to citizens; legislatures and elected representatives are important vehicles through which citizens and civic groups can also extract enforcement. Diagram 2.4 presents the newer types of accountability, highlighting the principal institutional actors and the accountability relations between them while Diagram 2.5 synthesises Diagrams 2.3 and 2.4 and highlights the oversight tools available to legislatures to promote the different types of accountability. It should be noted that legislatures are one of the institutions through which all forms of accountability can be exercised. In the next chapter, we examine the oversight tools available to the legislature to promote each type of accountability.

Summary and conclusion

In this chapter, we demonstrated that the subject of legislative oversight is under-theorised. We draw upon a variety of *neo-institutional* theories to explain the relationship between legislative oversight and corruption and democracy.

We drew first on *principal-agent theory* to explain the relationship between citizens, the executive and the legislature and how legislatures have adopted a variety of oversight tools to help them (as principals) hold the executive and the bureaucracy (as agents) to account. However, the empirical analysis in Chapters 4–6 suggests that one needs to look beyond institutional design and structural factors to explain variations in legislative oversight, democracy and corruption, across countries. It is pertinent to consider why there is a difference between parliamentary and presidential systems regarding

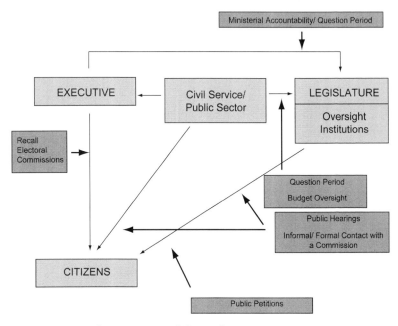

Diagram 2.5 Legislature's accountability tools

use of oversight tools and to what extent these differences might be explained through analytical lenses. Using these different approaches or theoretical lenses, we start to unpack the relationship between legislative oversight on the one hand and both democracy and corruption on the other hand. We also considered the role that legislative oversight tools are used in the promotion of different forms of accountability. In doing so, we expand the debate of the legislative oversight in the academic literature. While first-generation studies equated oversight capacity or potential to oversight activity, which, in its turn, was equated to effective oversight, the data analyses presented throughout this book make it quite clear that oversight effectiveness is not necessarily or, at least, not exclusively, a function of oversight activity (oversight activity can be performed on a large scale but may not be effective) and it is also equally clear that oversight activity is not necessarily a function of oversight capacity because the simple presence of oversight tools and mechanisms at the disposal of the legislature does not imply in any way that such tools will actually be put to any use. Hence, what we need to understand is not under what conditions and why political actors sometimes decide to use oversight mechanisms and to use them effectively. This is precisely what we plan to explain in Chapter 7, when we introduce and discuss at some length our strategic interaction model. Before doing so, in the next chapter, we consider the different types of legislative oversight tools and their distribution globally.

3 Legislative oversight tools

Introduction

In Chapter 2, we considered the theoretical foundations of legislative oversight, noting the importance of both agency and institutional theories. In this chapter, we focus on the oversight tools available to the legislature and on how they are distributed in countries with different forms of government, levels of democracy and levels of socioeconomic development. Diagram 3.1 highlights these tools and their authorship. These tools are the independent variables for the large-scale statistical analyses presented in Chapters 4–5 and the case study in Chapter 6. Within the context of ex-ante and ex-post oversight in the United States, Ogul (1976) suggested seven "opportunity factors" that promote or limit the potential for oversight. These are: legal authority or obligation, adequate staff, importance of the policy being overseen, the legislative committee system and its status within the legislature, the scope of oversight given executive–legislative relations, political party influences and the priorities of individual legislators. Olson and Mezey (1991), Olson and Norton (1996), Norton and Ahmed (1999) and Crowther and Olson (2002) go further, distinguishing between internal factors that influence oversight and external or contextual factors.

Wang (2005) usefully proposed a diagrammatic framework for studying these variables, which we present in Diagram 3.1. Nevertheless, she, as well as other scholars such as Olson and Mezey (1991), point out the difficulty in distinguishing between internal and external factors.[1] To take into account other oversight tools that she overlooked or excluded, we modify Wang's framework to take into account the additional factors identified by other scholars. We present this modified framework in Diagram 3.2.

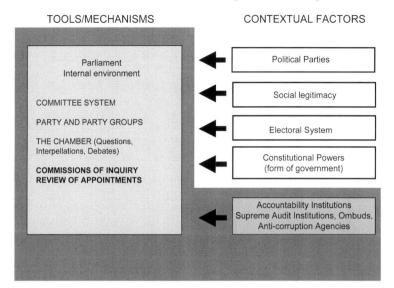

TOOLS/MECHANISMS CONTEXTUAL FACTORS

Diagram 3.1 Legislative oversight factors: Wang's framework

This chapter comprises three sections. In the first, we consider the various oversight tools used by legislatures. We differentiate between external and internal oversight tools. In so doing, we use our modified version of Wang's framework (Diagram 3.2). We go on to consider *external* oversight tools – supreme audit institutions (SAIs), ombuds offices and anti-corruption agencies. Then, we review *internal* oversight tools, namely, committees and special commissions of inquiry, confirmation of appointments, no confidence, censure and impeachment, questions and interpellations and debates in plenary. In the second section, we consider the distribution of legislative oversight tools globally. We present the results of the Inter-Parliamentary

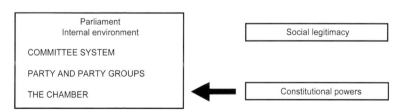

Diagram 3.2 Parliament internal environment
Source: Wang (2005: 16)

Union (IPU)/World Bank Institute (WBI) survey conducted in 2009. Specific attention is paid to the distribution of oversight tools in countries with different forms of government (that is, presidential, semi-presidential and parliamentary) together with the institutional correlates of this distribution. We also consider the distribution of oversight tools in upper chambers. In the third section, we present some conclusions.

Section one: legislative oversight tools

External oversight tools

Evans (1999: 1) describes extra-legislative accountability institutions as a diverse set of institutions designed "to enhance accountability of government, which operate outside parliament and the political process expressed through parliament", and whose creation paradoxically has been "largely driven by a perception of the inadequacy of parliament as an accountability mechanism". The literature distinguishes three such institutions: supreme audit institutions (SAIs), anti-corruption agencies and ombuds offices.[2] We consider each in turn.

Supreme audit institutions

SAIs undertake financial, legal (compliance) and, often, performance ("value-for-money") audits of government revenue and spending – work that is essential to the legislature's ex-post oversight of government accounts.

The relationship between legislatures and SAIs is often symbiotic (Stapenhurst and Titsworth, 2001). The legislature depends on the SAI submitting reliable and timely information, while the SAI depends on the legislature to provide a public forum for presenting and discussing audit results and any recommendations for corrective action. In many countries the constitution requires SAIs to report to the legislature – thereby ensuring independence. The legislature approves the SAI's budget and often appoints, or is required to approve the appointment of, the Auditor-General. Especially in Westminster parliamentary systems, the SAI works closely with a dedicated legislative committee (e.g. the Public Accounts Committee [PAC], state audit committee, budget or finance committee) or sub-committee and may even provide the committees with special technical assistance. This assistance might include preparing legislative proposals on state auditing, financial management or matters that have been the subject of major audits (Mazur and Vella, 2001, 2003).

There are three broad external audit models: the Westminster model (also known as the Anglo-Saxon or parliamentary model), the board or collegiate model and the judicial or Napoleonic model (Stapenhurst and Titsworth, 2001). Recent research on SAIs indicates that perceived corruption levels are significantly higher in countries in which the SAIs are a Court of Accounts (Blume and Voight, 2007).

Anti-corruption agencies

Many countries have established anti-corruption agencies, but their performance is generally disappointing (Meagher, 2004). There are four models of anti-corruption agencies: the *universal model*, which combines investigative, preventative and communications functions; the *investigative model*, which is characterised by a small and centralised investigative commission; the *multi-agency model*, which includes several offices across government departments that are individually distinct but together form a web of agencies to curb corruption; and the *parliamentary model*, which includes anti-corruption agencies that report directly to parliament and are independent from the executive and judicial branches of state (Heilbrunn, 2004: 3).

While anti-corruption agencies could play an important role in reducing corruption, they are often "captured" by the government to protect its own leadership and/or to harass opposition leaders.[3] There have been no cross-country analyses of the effectiveness of such agencies in curbing corruption. Nevertheless, as is the case with other external accountability institutions, it can be hypothesised that anti-corruption agencies are most effective when independent of government and free of political interference regarding their operations.

Ombuds offices

Originally developed in Sweden in 1809, the ombuds office[4] represents the interests of the public by investigating and addressing complaints reported by individual citizens against public authorities. In some countries ombuds offices have mandates that go beyond oversight of legality and good governance – to include human rights and mediation between citizens and public authorities. Less typical is an explicit anti-corruption mandate, such as that found in Papua New Guinea, Uganda and Namibia.

In some countries (e.g. Belgium), the ombuds office may investigate a particular administration at the legislature's request. Furthermore, the impetus for legislative oversight may be reinforced by the ombuds office, ensuring that information from its investigations is widely available to the media and the general public.

The decisions of the ombuds offices in most countries are not binding and their powers to act reside more in the realms of mediation and conciliation, providing guidance, making recommendations and issuing reprimands. Only in a few countries (e.g. Finland, Sweden) do ombuds offices have the power to initiate criminal prosecutions, although the legislature itself may follow-up where there is a legislative ombuds committee.

Internal oversight tools

Scholars have identified four internal oversight tools: (i) committees and special commissions of inquiry; (ii) review of appointments and power to censure/impeach/dismiss; (iii) chamber proceedings: questions and interpellations; and (iv) chamber, or plenary, debates. We review each in turn.

Committees and special commissions of inquiry

Joseph LaPalombara (1974: 311) held that "if the national legislature is to be a significant political factor, then it must have specialized committees of limited membership and considerable scope of power". Wehner (2004: 13) calls committees "the engine room" of the legislature … [where] in-depth and technical debate can take place, away from the political grandstanding that often characterizes proceedings in the chamber". The outcome of a committee's investigations typically takes the form of a report to the legislature, which is also published. The report and its recommendations may be debated in the plenary, and the legislature may require a response or follow-up actions from the government.

While all committees perform some level of oversight, some legislatures have established specialised audit or PACs, which work closely with the SAI. Such committees can enhance ex-post budget oversight and complement the policy oversight of other committees.

In some legislatures, such as those in Nigeria, Bulgaria and some Australian states, anti-corruption committees have also been established to work closely with anti-corruption agencies.

Political parties often have significant influence on the functioning of committees and strong party discipline and/or single-party dominance may weaken committees and their oversight potential. Membership independence is often a contentious issue, as the ruling party may seek to remove members seen as being too "critical". Dubrow (2001: 26) argues that

> In parliamentary systems ... the domination of committees by members of the governing party significantly limits the effectiveness of parliamentary oversight. Frequent turnover of progovernment committee members by the governing party can also weaken the cumulative knowledge of the committee ... [and prevent] members from acquiring any significant policy expertise.

Examining legislative oversight in post-communist countries, Olson (2004: 19) concurs, noting that "opportunities for committees to engage in administrative review and oversight increase to the extent that single party control is relaxed". Similarly, as single-party dominance has decreased in Ghana and Kenya, their parliaments have become more effective in their oversight activities (Africa Report, 2006).

Committees' outreach activities can help forge synergy between people's awareness and concerns, and the oversight function of parliament, thus creating the linkage between legislative oversight and public engagement that has been noted, but not developed, by the World Bank. Yamamoto (2008) notes that 71 out of 88 reporting legislatures have procedures for holding public hearings and receiving submissions from the public.

In addition, committees may try and make up for insufficient staff by going to outside specialists from civil society and academia. Civil society organisations often assist legislatures and their committees in budget oversight. For example, the Uganda Debt Network has helped to monitor and correct serious leakages occurring in the transfer of funds from the National Ministry of Finance to individual schools. South Africa's Public Sector Accountability Monitor (PSAM) works closely with the legislature to track the executive branch's response to allegations of misconduct contained in the Auditor General's report (Krafchik, 2003).

Apart from regular committees, the legislature may set up *special commissions of inquiry*, or investigation committees, to examine issues of public concern and to make recommendations on current and future policies and legislation. Such commissions are time-bound and their subjects typically cut across the responsibilities of several government agencies or departments and several parliamentary committees. Such commissions are usually empowered to summon witnesses to testify under oath, including officials of the executive branch, and to demand documents and order on-site inspections. Hearings to gather evidence may be held in public. In some countries they have even broader powers of investigation, similar to those of the investigating magistrate or prosecutor (OECD, 2001).[5] At the end of their investigation, the commissions generally issue a report to the full chamber or to the public. Countries that have established such commissions to examine corruption include Kenya (Matiangi, 2006), Peru (BBC, 2001), São Tomé and Principe (Chabal *et al.*, 2002) and Brazil (BBC, 2005).

Confirmation of appointments, no confidence, censure and impeachment

Another oversight power lies in whether the legislature plays a role in executive appointments. The legislature's authority may vary – from the power to reject a candidate to a more advisory role (NDI, 2000). Confirmation of executive appointments is more common in presidential systems (e.g. South Korea, Nigeria, the Philippines and the United States), and tends to involve comprehensive investigations of the executive's proposed candidate. Some semi-presidential and parliamentary systems also have procedures for oversight of appointments of high-ranking senior civil servants (IPU, 2006).

Even after executive and judicial officials have been appointed, the legislature may have the power to remove or impeach them. Some parliamentary systems also allow for no-confidence votes on individual ministers; such votes are not considered a referendum on overall government policies, but rather on that person's performance in office (NDI, 2000). The *threat* of a vote of no confidence, more common than votes of no confidence themselves, may also lead individual ministers to resign.

In some countries the legislature has the power to remove the government from office, either through impeachment or a vote of no confidence. Impeachment, again more commonly found in presidential systems, is used as a last resort, when the president is seen to have committed a significant breach of the law or constitution (NDI, 2000). In parliamentary systems, a vote of no confidence is more likely to indicate a loss of political support than illegal actions on the part of the government (IPU, 2006).

The chamber: questions and interpellations

The right to question ministers, both orally and in writing, is among the traditional forms of oversight in both parliamentary systems and semi-presidential systems, where ministers are also members of the legislature. Originally developed in the United Kingdom, this practice can now be found in legislatures worldwide (NDI, 2000).[6] Questions are used to obtain information, request government action to solve problems, criticise government, expose abuses and seek redress. Answering publicly for any potential shortcomings is seen as an important contribution to accountability and is the direct consequence of ministerial responsibility and accountability to the legislature (Mulgan, 2003).

Interpellations are similar to parliamentary questions, but often more formal and extensive, "designed to provoke comprehensive debate on an issue or a particular case of ministerial neglect" (NDI, 2000). Some parliaments require more than one member to file an interpellation – for example, a parliamentary group of at least 34 members in Germany, and at least 10 legislators from two party factions in India (NDI, 2000). In Finland, interpellations are generally made by the opposition parties and require the signature of at least 20 MPs.

Ultimately, the effectiveness of questions and interpellations may rest upon parliament's power to sanction government by censuring individual ministers or dismissing them or the government. Interpellations sometimes end with a formal resolution or a motion that the minister should resign, although these rarely pass in legislatures with government majorities (NDI, 2000).

Chamber: debates in plenary[7]

Yamamoto (2008: 62) defines debates in plenary as " ... oral exchanges of opinion that are intended to facilitate the chamber's collective decision-making on certain issues". They can, he suggests, " ... take place on special occasions, such as opening speeches or at different stages of draft legislation [and can] address issues that are chosen by parliamentarians themselves or highlight the work of parliamentary committees". The effectiveness of plenary debates as an oversight mechanism is influenced by the time allowed for debates, whether the opposition has reserved time for debates on subjects of its choosing, whether the debates are open to the public, the degree of non-partisanship and professionalism on the part of the presiding officers and so on.[8]

In Westminster parliamentary systems, not only are there "opposition" days, when the opposition leader determines which debates will take place, but there are also debates on adjournment, which are held at the end of every session and are typically initiated by an individual parliamentarian. It is common for such debates to focus on problems in constituencies or on individual complaints rather than on national issues, such as corruption (Yamamoto, 2008).

Section two: distribution of oversight tools

In this section, we present the results of a new survey conducted in 2009 by WBI in collaboration with the IPU, to see whether and to what extent the findings presented in earlier studies are validated by the results of this new survey, conducted eight years later. Specific attention is be paid to three sets of issues that were extensively discussed following the earlier survey, namely the distribution of oversight tools in countries with different forms of government (that is, parliamentary, semi-presidential and presidential) together with the institutional correlates of this distribution.

We first provide an overview of the 2009 survey, including when it was administered, by whom, to whom, and what the content of the questionnaire was. This allows us to appreciate differences and similarities between the 2001 and the 2009 survey instruments. We then focus on the distribution of oversight tools in different legislatures. In doing so, we will pay attention to which tools are available to which legislatures, to how many tools are available to each of the legislatures, and to whether these new findings validate the results of previous analyses. The analysis of the 2009 survey data reveals, consistent with what has already been argued in the literature, three sets of findings, namely: (i) that all legislatures have at least one oversight tool and usually more than one; (ii) that some oversight tools are more common than others; and (iii) that the distribution of tools in 2009 is very consistent with that recorded in 2001. Subsequently, we investigate the institutional correlates of the distribution of tools of legislative oversight. Here we show that, as previous studies had indicated, the number of oversight tools available to legislatures varies across forms of government. On average, the highest number of oversight tools is to be found in parliamentary systems and the lowest in presidential ones; the number of oversight tools available to legislatures in semi-presidential settings falls between these two extremes. Then we address one of the findings presented by Pelizzo and Stapenhurst (2008), namely that legislatures in developed nations have, on average, more oversight tools at their disposal than legislatures in developing nations, subject to empirical verification. We go on to discuss how oversight tools are distributed across various levels of democracy, and finally we compare the oversight capacity in lower and upper chambers. By so doing we are be able to highlight some of the similarities and the differences in the oversight capacity and the distribution of oversight tools. In the final section we present some tentative conclusions.

i) *The 2009 survey*
The IPU-WBI survey conducted in 2009 asked 80 questions, covering a variety of issues such as the presence/absence of specific oversight tools, mechanisms for the oversight of policy implementation, the role of the legislature in the budget process and the presence/absence of codes of legislative conduct. Hence, we focus only on questions and responses related to legislative oversight of the government. Specifically, respondents were asked whether, in exercising oversight of the government, a legislature can employ oral and written questions, interpellations, motions for debate, hearings in committees, set up committees of inquiry, draft reports, send missions to the government departments, and whether there is an ombudsman.

The survey was sent to all member legislatures (both upper and lower chambers) of the IPU, and responses were received from 97 lower chambers and 19 upper chambers. We focus mainly on the oversight tools available to lower chambers, although in the final part of the chapter we broaden our analysis to include oversight tools used in upper chambers.

ii) *The distribution of oversight tools*
The data presented in tables 3.1 through 3.3 suggest three sets of considerations. First, they make clear that all countries adopt some

Table 3.1 Tools of legislative oversight in lower chambers

Country	Oral and Written Questions	Interpellations	Motions for Debate	Hearings in Committee	Committees of Inquiry	Missions to Government departments concerned	Reports	Ombudsman
Algeria	yes	yes	yes	yes	yes	no	no	no
Andorra	yes	no	yes	yes	yes	no	yes	yes
Antigua and Barbuda	yes	yes	yes	yes	yes	no	yes	yes
Argentina	yes	yes	no	yes	yes	no	yes	yes
Armenia	yes	yes	yes	yes	no	no	yes	yes
Austria	yes	yes	yes	yes	yes	no	yes	yes
Bahrain	yes	yes	no	yes	yes	yes	no	no
Bangladesh	yes	yes	yes	yes	yes	yes	yes	yes
Benin, Republic of	yes	yes	yes	yes	yes	yes	no	yes
Bhutan	yes	yes	yes	yes	yes	no	no	no
Bulgaria	yes	yes	yes	yes	yes	no	yes	no
Burkina Faso	yes	yes	yes	yes	yes	yes	yes	yes
Burundi	yes	yes	yes	yes	yes	yes	no	no
Cambodia	yes	no	no	yes	no	no	no	no
Cameroon	yes	yes	yes	no	yes	no	no	no
Canada	yes	no	yes	yes	yes	no	yes	no
Central African Republic	yes	yes	no	yes	yes	no	no	yes
Chile	yes	yes	no	yes	no	no	yes	n.a.
Congo, Democratic Republic of	yes	yes	yes	yes	yes	yes	yes	yes

Table 3.1 (continued)

Country	Oral and Written Questions	Interpellations	Motions for Debate	Hearings in Committee	Committees of Inquiry	Missions to Government departments concerned	Reports	Ombudsman
Costa Rica	yes	yes	yes	yes	yes	no	yes	yes
Côte d'Ivoire	yes	no	no	no	yes	no	no	yes
Croatia	yes	yes	no	no	yes	no	yes	yes
Cyprus	yes	no	no	yes	yes	no	yes	yes
Czech Republic	yes	yes	yes	yes	yes	yes	yes	yes
Djibouti	yes	yes	no	yes	yes	yes	yes	yes
Estonia	yes	yes	no	yes	yes	no	yes	yes
Finland	yes	yes	yes	yes	yes	no	yes	yes
France	yes	no	no	yes	yes	yes	yes	yes
Gabon	yes	yes	no	yes	yes	yes	yes	yes
Georgia	yes	yes	yes	yes	yes	no	yes	yes
Germany	yes	yes	no	yes	yes	no	yes	no
Ghana	yes	no	yes	yes	yes	no	no	yes
Greece	yes	yes	yes	yes	yes	no	yes	yes
Grenada	yes	yes	yes	yes	yes	no	no	yes
Haiti	yes	yes	no	yes	yes	yes	yes	yes
Hungary	yes	yes	yes	yes	yes	no	yes	yes
Iceland	yes	no	no	yes	yes	no	yes	yes
Indonesia	yes	yes	no	yes	yes	yes	no	yes
Ireland	yes	no	yes	yes	yes	no	yes	yes
Iran, Islamic Republic of	yes	yes	yes	yes	yes	no	yes	yes
Israel	yes	yes	no	yes	yes	no	no	yes

Table 3.1 (continued)

Country	Oral and Written Questions	Interpellations	Motions for Debate	Hearings in Committee	Committees of Inquiry	Missions to Government departments concerned	Reports	Ombudsman
Jamaica	yes	yes	yes	yes	yes	yes	yes	yes
Japan	yes	no	no	yes	yes	yes	yes	no
Jordan	yes	yes	yes	yes	yes	yes	yes	yes
Kenya	yes	yes	yes	yes	yes	yes	yes	yes
Korea, Republic of	yes	yes	no	yes	yes	no	yes	no
Latvia	yes	yes	no	yes	yes	yes	yes	yes
Lebanon	yes	yes	yes	no	yes	no	no	yes
Lesotho	no	no	yes	yes	no	yes	yes	yes
Liberia	yes	no	yes	yes	yes	yes	yes	n.a.
Liechtenstein	yes	yes	yes	yes	yes	yes	yes	yes
Lithuania	yes	yes	yes	yes	yes	yes	yes	yes
Luxembourg	yes	yes	no	yes	yes	no	no	yes
Macedonia	yes	yes	no	yes	yes	no	no	yes
Malaysia	yes	yes	yes	yes	yes	yes	yes	no
Marshall Islands	yes	no	yes	yes	yes	no	yes	no
Mauritius	yes	no	yes	yes	yes	no	no	yes
Moldova, Republic of	yes	yes	no	yes	no	no	yes	yes
Monaco	yes	no	no	yes	no	no	no	yes
Morocco	yes	yes	yes	yes	yes	yes	yes	yes
Namibia	yes	yes	yes	yes	yes	yes	yes	yes
Netherlands	yes	yes	yes	yes	yes	no	yes	yes
New Zealand	yes	no	yes	yes	yes	no	yes	yes

Table 3.1 (continued)

Country	Oral and Written Questions	Interpellations	Motions for Debate	Hearings in Committee	Committees of Inquiry	Missions to Government departments concerned	Reports	Ombudsman
Nicaragua	no	yes	no	yes	yes	no	yes	yes
Norway	yes	yes	yes	yes	yes	no	no	yes
Palau	yes	no	no	yes	yes	no	yes	yes
Paraguay	no	yes	yes	yes	yes	no	yes	yes
Philippines	yes	yes	no	yes	yes	no	no	yes
Poland	yes	yes	yes	yes	yes	no	yes	yes
Qatar	yes	no	no	no	no	no	no	yes
Romania	yes	yes	yes	yes	yes	no	no	yes
San Marino	yes	yes	yes	yes	yes	no	yes	no
Senegal	yes	no	yes	yes	yes	yes	yes	yes
Serbia	yes	yes	yes	yes	yes	no	yes	yes
Seychelles	yes	no	yes	yes	yes	no	no	yes
Singapore	yes	no	yes	yes	yes	yes	yes	no
Slovakia	yes	yes	no	yes	no	yes	yes	yes
Slovenia	yes	yes	yes	yes	yes	no	yes	yes
Spain	yes	yes	yes	yes	yes	no	yes	yes
Sri Lanka	yes	no	yes	Yes	yes	no	yes	yes
Sweden	yes	yes	yes	Yes	yes	yes	yes	yes
Switzerland	yes	yes	yes	Yes	yes	no	yes	yes
Tajikistan	no	no	no	No	no	no	yes	yes
Tanzania, United Republic of	yes	yes	yes	Yes	yes	yes	yes	yes
Thailand	yes	yes	yes	Yes	no	no	no	yes

Table 3.1 (continued)

Country	Oral and Written Questions	Interpellations	Motions for Debate	Hearings in Committee	Committees of Inquiry	Missions to Government departments concerned	Reports	Ombudsman
Togo	yes	yes	no	Yes	yes	yes	no	no
Tonga	yes	yes	yes	Yes	yes	yes	yes	yes
Trinidad and Tobago	yes	no	yes	Yes	yes	no	yes	yes
Tunisia	yes	yes	no	Yes	no	yes	yes	yes
Turkey	yes	yes	yes	Yes	no	no	no	no
Uganda	no	no	no	No	yes	no	no	yes
Ukraine	yes	yes	yes	Yes	yes	yes	yes	yes
United Kingdom	yes	yes	yes	Yes	yes	no	no	yes
Uruguay	yes	yes	yes	Yes	yes	yes	yes	yes
Vietnam	yes	yes	yes	Yes	yes	yes	yes	yes
Yemen, Republic of	yes	yes	yes	Yes	no	no	no	no
Zimbabwe	yes	no	yes	Yes	yes	yes	yes	yes

tools of legislative oversight, as the analysis of the 2001 IPU-WBI data had previously indicated. Specifically, the data collected in 2009 reveal that all of the 97 lower chambers for which information was collected report to have two or more tools and that almost 90 per cent of the lower chambers have 5 tools or more. On average, they have 6 oversight tools at their disposal – a value slightly higher than the average recorded (admittedly with a different survey questionnaire) in 2001, when it was found that legislatures had on average 5.49 oversight tools at their disposal.[9]

Second, the data generated by the more recent survey make it clear that there is, as the analysis of the 2001 survey had previously indicated, some variation in how common the various tools are. The analysis using the 2001 survey data indicated that committee hearings, questions and the creation of inquiry committees were the three most common tools of legislative oversight, as they were found in about 91 per cent of the countries covered in the survey. The other tools, in order of popular usage, were hearings in plenary sittings of the legislature, question time, interpellations and the ombudsman. The analysis of the 2009 survey data displays a very similar picture: questions (oral and written), committee hearings and the creation of committees of inquiry are the three most common oversight tools. While no evidence was gathered on question time and hearings in the plenary, the 2009 survey showed that ombudsmen and interpellations are less common than questions, hearings and inquiry committees, but more common than reports, motions and missions to the government. Details can be found in table 3.2.[10]

The third consideration suggested by the more recent data is that despite the fact that the questionnaire used in 2009 differs somewhat from the questionnaire used in 2001, and that there is only a limited overlap between the countries covered by the 2001 survey and those covered by the 2009 survey, the findings of the two surveys are largely consistent: the average number of tools estimated by the two surveys is approximately the same, they both indicated that questions are the most common oversight tool, the percentage of respondents reporting to have a specific tool in 2009 is extremely close to the percentage found in 2001. (See table 3.3).

iii) *Oversight tools and form of government*
While the evidence presented in the previous section supports the claim that there is considerable variation in the number of oversight

Table 3.2 Use of oversight tools by percentage of respondents (N = 97)

Oral and Written Questions	Interpellations	Motions for Debate	Hearings in Committee	Committees of Inquiry	Missions to Government departments concerned	Reports	Ombudsman
96.8	74.7	67.4	94.7	88.4	37.9	71.6	81.1

Table 3.3 Country ordering by number of oversight tools

Two	Three	Four	Five	Six	Seven	Eight
Cambodia	Côte d'Ivoire	Cameroon	Algeria	Andorra	Antigua and Barbuda	Bangladesh
Qatar	Monaco	Chile	Bahrain	Argentina	Austria	Burkina Faso
Tajikistan		Turkey	Bhutan	Armenia	Benin, Republic of	Congo, Democratic Republic of
Uganda		Yemen, Republic of	Canada	Bulgaria	Costa Rica	Czech Republic
			Central African Republic	Burundi	Djibouti	Jamaica
			Croatia	Estonia	Finland	Jordan
			Cyprus	France	Gabon	Kenya
			Germany	Grenada	Georgia	Liechtenstein
			Ghana	Indonesia	Greece	Lithuania
			Iceland	Ireland	Haiti	Morocco
			Israel	Liberia	Hungary	Namibia
			Japan	New Zealand	Iran, Islamic Republic of	Sweden
			Korea, Republic of	Norway	Latvia	Tanzania, United Republic of

Table 3.3 (continued)

Two	Three	Four	Five	Six	Seven	Eight
			Lebanon	Paraguay	Malaysia	Tonga
			Lesotho	Romania	Netherlands	Ukraine
			Luxembourg	San Marino	Poland	Uruguay
			Macedonia	Singapore	Senegal	Vietnam
			Marshall Islands	Slovakia	Serbia	
			Mauritius	Sri Lanka	Slovenia	
			Moldova,	Trinidad and	Spain	
			Republic of	Tobago		
			Nicaragua	Tunisia	Switzerland	
			Palau	United Kingdom	Zimbabwe	
			Philippines			
			Seychelles			
			Thailand			
			Togo			

tools that legislatures can employ to oversee government activities, it does not say much as to why there is such a variation. Previous studies showed that the number of oversight tools available to a legislature is significantly affected by the institutional/constitutional design of the country in which the legislature operates. Specifically, Pelizzo and Stapenhurst (2008) found that, on average, legislatures in countries with a parliamentary form of government had the highest number of oversight tools (6.35 on average) at their disposal, that legislatures in countries with a presidential form of government had the lowest number of tools (5.69) and that legislatures in countries with a semi-presidential form of government fell somewhere in between these two extremes, with 5.71 tools. The analysis of the 2009 survey data displays a very similar picture: legislatures in presidential systems have on average 5.68 oversight tools – almost precisely the same as they had in the 2001 survey; legislatures in semi-presidential regimes have on average 6.13 oversight tools (up from 5.71 in 2001); and legislatures in countries with parliamentary systems have on average 6.28 oversight tools (down somewhat from the 6.35 oversight tools recorded in 2001). (See table 3.4).[11]

iv) *Distribution of oversight tools and income level*
Previous work (Pelizzo and Stapenhurst, 2008) showed that the average number of tools available to a legislature to oversee the activities of the executive was strongly related to the level of socio-economic development of the country in which a legislature operates. However, we also found that countries with the highest incomes have the least number of oversight tools available. Legislatures in low-income countries had on average 5.5 tools, legislatures in middle-income countries had on average 6.25 oversight tools and legislatures in high-income countries had on average 6.27 oversight tools.

The results of the 2009 survey present a somewhat different picture. Legislatures in low-income countries have fewer tools than legislature in the middle- and high-income countries. However, while legislatures in high-income OECD countries have more oversight tools than legislatures in other (non-OECD) high-income countries and in lower-middle-income countries, they have as many tools as legislatures in upper-middle-income countries. The fact that legislatures in upper-middle-income have more tools than legislatures in high-income non-OECD countries has a major impact on the results: when we aggregate the distribution of oversight tools by the three income levels used by

Table 3.4 The distribution of oversight tools by form of government

Form of Government	Number of Tools						
	Two	Three	Four	Five	Six	Seven	Eight
Presidential	Tajikistan	Côte d'Ivoire	Chile Yemen, Republic of	Bahrain Cyprus Germany Korea, Republic of Marshall Islands Moldova, Republic of Nicaragua Seychelles	Argentina Armenia Burundi Indonesia Liberia Paraguay Philippines Sri Lanka Tunisia	Benin, Republic of Costa Rica Djibouti Georgia Iran, Islamic Republic of Serbia	Congo, Democratic Republic of Namibia
Parliamentary			Turkey	Canada Croatia Iceland Israel Japan	Bulgaria Estonia Grenada Ireland Norway	Antigua and Barbuda Austria Finland Greece Hungary	Bangladesh Czech Republic Jamaica Lithuania Tanzania, United Republic of

Table 3.4 (continued)

Form of Government	Number of Tools						
	Two	Three	Four	Five	Six	Seven	Eight
				Lebanon Macedonia Mauritius	San Marino Singapore Slovakia Trinidad and Tobago United Kingdom	Latvia Poland Slovenia Zimbabwe	Uruguay Vietnam
Semi-Presidential			Cameroon	Algeria Central African Republic	France	Gabon Haiti Romania Senegal	Burkina Faso
Parliamentary/ Monarchy	Cambodia Qatar			Bhutan Lesotho Luxembourg Thailand	New Zealand	Malaysia Netherlands Spain	Jordan Liechtenstein Morocco Sweden Tonga
Other	Uganda	Monaco		Ghana Palau Togo	Andorra	Switzerland	Kenya Ukraine

Table 3.5a The distribution of oversight tools by income level

Income Level	Number of Oversight Tools 2	3	4	5	6	7	8	Total	Mean
Low	3		1	3	2	4	6	19	5.95
Lower-middle		1	1	6	6	3	4	21	6.00
Upper-middle			2	6	4	6	4	22	6.18
High	1		1	11	10	9	3	35	5.91
Total	4		2	4	26	22	22	17	97

Table 3.5b Distribution of oversight tools in high-income countries: OECD v. non-OECD

	2	3	4	5	6	7	8	Total	Mean
OECD	0	0	0	6	6	7	2	21	6.24
Non-OECD	1	1	0	4	5	2	1	14	5.5

Pelizzo and Stapenhurst (2008) we find that legislatures in middle-income countries have a greater oversight capacity than legislatures in either low- or high-income countries.

v) *Distribution of oversight tools across levels of democracy*
In order to assess whether and to what extent the distribution of oversight tools is related to the quality of democracy, we proceed in the following way. Using the 2009 Gastil index scores for each of the countries included in the survey, we identify three types of countries: liberal democracies, formal democracies and non-democracies. The first group of countries (liberal democracies) cover the countries that have a Gastil score of 1 through 3, the second group (formal democracies) are countries that have a score of 3.5 through 5, while the third group includes countries that are regarded as non-democratic and that score 5.5 or more in the Gastil index.

Having identified these three types of countries we create three dichotomous variables. The liberal democracy variable takes value 1 for the 55 countries whose Gastil index score is between 1 and 3 and takes value 0 otherwise; the formal democracy variable takes value 1 for the 28 countries that score between 3.5 and 5 and takes value 0 otherwise; while the non-democracy variable takes value 1 for countries that score 5.5 or more in the Gastil index and takes value 0 otherwise. When this kind of analysis was performed by Pelizzo and Stapenhurst (2008), the analysis was conducted with a much smaller sample. The sample employed by Pelizzo and Stapenhurst (2008: 20) included 49 cases – 27 liberal democracies, 14 formal democracies and 8 non-democracies. By using that sample, we found that in 2001 liberal democracies had on average 6.41 oversight tools, that formal democracies had on average 5.71 oversight tools and that non-democracies had on average 5 oversight tools. In other words, we found that legislatures in countries that were more democratic had more tools than countries that were less democratic.

When we use the 2009 survey data, however, we get somewhat different results. First of all, while the number of oversight tools available to non-democratic countries in 2009 is virtually identical to the number of tools at their disposal in 2001, the number of tools available to both liberal and formal democracies has changed. The number of oversight tools available to formal democracies has increased to 6.13 (from 5.71), while the number of tools available to parliaments in liberal democracies has declined to 6.15 (from 6.41). Second, while parliaments in both liberal and formal democracies have more oversight tools than parliaments operating in non-democratic settings, as previous studies had already indicated, the more recent data reveal that legislatures in formal democracies have almost as many oversight tools at their disposal as legislatures in liberal democratic countries. (See data in table 3.6).

vi) *Oversight tools in lower and upper chambers: a comparison*
The data presented in tables 3.7 through 3.9 provide some information as to which tools are available to upper chamber, which tools

Table 3.6 Distribution of oversight tools by level of democracy

	Two	Three	Four	Five	Six	Seven	Eight	Mean
Liberal democracy	0	1	1	13	14	13	6	6.15
Formal democracy	1	0	2	12	7	7	9	6.13
Non-democracy	3	1	1	1	1	2	2	4.91

are most common and how they are distributed across various forms of government.

The data at our disposal indicate that upper chambers are, on average, less equipped to oversee the executive than lower chambers. (See table 3.7).

Second, the data reveal that while all upper chambers employ some oversight tools (questions and hearings in committees), other oversight tools are relatively less popular. While missions, reports and motions were the least common tools in the lower chambers, the least common tools in the upper chambers are missions, motions and interpellations. (See table 3.8).

Third, the data reveal that there is quite some variation in the number of oversight tools available to upper chambers across various forms of government. In this respect, we find that while upper chambers in presidential settings have on average only 5.75 oversight tools, upper chambers in semi-presidential and parliamentary systems have respectively 6.5 and 6.77 oversight tools. In other words, upper chambers in parliamentary systems are the best equipped to oversee the government activities, upper chambers in presidential systems are the worst equipped to oversee the executive while upper chambers in the semi-presidential systems fall somewhere in between. (See table 3.9).

These findings, as will be recalled, are perfectly consistent with what previous studies had reported (Pelizzo and Stapenhurst, 2004; Pelizzo and Stapenhurst, 2008) where it was noted that legislatures in parliamentary systems have the greatest capacity to oversee the executive followed by the legislatures in semi-presidential settings and by legislatures operating in countries with a presidential regime.

These findings are important for another reason, as they may help us understand why the average oversight capacity of legislatures in 2009 seems to be lower than what it was in 2001. The reason is that in 2001 the oversight capacity of legislatures in parliamentary systems (as well as in the other systems) was assessed by analysing a dataset that combined the data pertaining to both the lower and the upper chamber. Here instead we have analysed the data pertaining to the lower chambers independently from the data from the upper chambers. If we combine the data for lower and upper chambers we find the number of oversight tools available to all reporting legislatures to be higher in 2009 (6.56 tools) compared with 6.35 tools in 2001.

Table 3.7 The tools of legislative oversight

Country	Oral and written questions	Interpellations	Motions for debate	Hearings in committee	Committees of inquiry	Missions to government departments concerned	Reports	Ombudsman
Afghanistan	yes	yes	yes	Yes	yes	yes	yes	no
Algeria	yes	yes	yes	Yes	yes	no	no	no
Australia	yes	no	yes	Yes	yes	no	yes	yes
Burundi	yes	no	no	Yes	yes	yes	no	yes
France	yes	no	no	Yes	yes	yes	yes	yes
Gabon	yes	yes	yes	yes	yes	yes	no	yes
Grenada	yes	yes	yes	yes	yes	no	no	yes
Haiti	yes	yes	no	yes	yes	yes	yes	yes
Jamaica	yes	yes	yes	yes	yes	yes	yes	yes
Japan	yes	yes	yes	yes	yes	yes	yes	no
Namibia	yes	yes	yes	yes	yes	yes	yes	yes
Pakistan	yes	no	yes	yes	yes	no	yes	yes
Romania	yes	yes	yes	yes	yes	no	yes	yes
Rwanda	yes	yes	no	yes	yes	yes	yes	yes
Slovakia	yes	yes	no	yes	no	yes	yes	yes
Spain	yes	yes	yes	yes	yes	no	yes	yes
United States of America	yes	no	no	yes	no	no	yes	no
Uruguay	yes	yes	yes	yes	yes	yes	yes	yes

Table 3.8 Use of oversight tools, by number of respondents

Oral and written questions	Interpellations	Motions for debate	Hearings in committee	Committees of inquiry	Missions to government departments concerned	Reports	Ombudsman
19	13	13	19	17	12	15	15

Table 3.9 Number of legislative oversight tools used by surveyed countries

Form of government	Number of tools					
	Three	Four	Five	Six	Seven	Eight
Presidential	United States of America		Burundi		Afghanistan	Namibia
Parliamentary				Australia Grenada Pakistan Slovakia	Japan Zimbabwe Spain	Jamaica Uruguay
Semi-Presidential			Algeria	France	Gabon Haiti Romania Rwanda	

Section three: conclusions

In this chapter, we first considered the array of oversight tools that have been developed by legislatures and are used by them to correct for some of the agency problems, noted in Chapter 2. We reviewed both external and insight/oversight tools, using our modification of Wang's (2005) framework for classifying oversight tools. Then, we went on to present the results of a survey conducted by WBI in collaboration with IPU among 97 lower chambers (and 19 upper chambers). The survey was almost entirely devoted to the collection of information on executive–legislative relations, on legislative oversight of the executive activities and on the role of the parliament in the budget process.

Building on the work of Pelizzo and Stapenhurst (2004, 2008), who presented the results of a survey conducted in 2001, we show that most of the findings discussed in that earlier work are corroborated by the results of this new survey. First, the distribution of oversight tools is consistent with what previous research had indicated with legislatures in parliamentary settings having more oversight tools at their disposal than legislatures operating in either presidential or semi-presidential systems. And second, legislatures operating in more democratic settings have on average more oversight tools than legislatures in less democratic ones. While these findings are consistent with and corroborate earlier research findings, our new analysis presented here reveals that the relationship between legislatures and oversight capacity may be more complex than had previously been thought. In fact, while previous work showed the average number of oversight tools available increased monotonically as income increased, the findings presented in this chapter tell quite a different story. The claim that legislatures in high-income countries have the highest number of oversight tools at their disposal is true only if one focuses on OECD countries, but it is not otherwise. In fact, the data presented in this chapter show that legislatures in high-income non-OCED countries actually have the lowest average number of oversight tools.

We now proceed to our large-scale statistical analyses of legislative oversight and the quality of democracy in the next chapter, and of legislative oversight and corruption in Chapter 5.

4 Legislative oversight and the quality of democracy

Introduction

Having considered the theoretical foundations of legislative oversight (in Chapter 2) and the types and global distribution of legislative oversight tools (in Chapter 3), in this chapter we show how and why that legislatures' oversight capacity should be significant determinant of the quality of democracy. We do so by applying Morlino's (2005) framework for the analysis of the quality of democracy. After arguing why oversight capacity should make a significant contribution to the quality of democracy by contributing to one of its sub-dimensions, we test whether this is indeed the case.

Building on a political-science literature that has long debated how the quality of democracy could be measured, benchmarked and assessed, Morlino (2005) suggests that any successful effort of measuring democracy should take into account the fact that democracy is a multi-dimensional phenomenon. Specifically, the notion of democratic quality could refer to: (i) the procedures employed by the democratic regime; (ii) the output of the democratic regime; and (iii) the outcome of the democratic regime, that is, whether it is stable and legitimate.

According to Morlino (2005), each of these macro-dimensions entails several sub-dimensions. The quality of democracy in terms of outcome can easily be assessed on the basis of whether a democratic regime is responsive to the citizens, whether it is perceived to be responsive or whether it is regarded as a legitimate one. The quality of democracy in terms of outputs can be assessed on the basis of whether and how well the democratic regime is able to promote socio-economic (as well as political) equality and to protect individual rights and freedoms. The quality of democracy in terms of procedures can be assessed on the basis of several sub-components such as the rule of law, participation, competition, electoral accountability and inter-institutional accountability.

Inter-institutional accountability refers to the legislature's (and to the judiciary's) ability to oversee the activities of the executive branch. And in so far as a legislature's ability to oversee the executive branch is facilitated by the range of oversight tools at its disposal, it is reasonable to hypothesise that legislatures which have more oversight tools at their disposal have a greater oversight capacity and that this greater oversight capacity is conducive to greater inter-institutional accountability and, ultimately, to a democracy of a higher quality.

The claim that stronger legislatures are good for democracy (e.g. Fish, 2006) provided much of the justification for legislative strengthening activities and programs undertaken by international organisations, bilateral donors and others. Typically, the primary goal of these organisations was either the promotion of either socio-economic development or the promotion of democracy. Both sets of organisations saw in the strengthening of legislatures' oversight capacity the way in which their objectives could be achieved. International organisations whose primary objective was poverty reduction and socio-economic development thought that legislatures with greater oversight capacity could be more effective in keeping government accountable for their actions and better able to promote good governance and curb corruption, thereby creating the conditions for sustainable socio-economic development.[1] International organisations devoted to democracy promotion, on the other hand, thought that stronger legislatures would contribute to the improvement of democratic quality and would be, therefore, good for democracy, its consolidation and ultimately its survival.

While in the next chapter we will investigate the relationship between legislatures' oversight capacity and corruption, in this chapter we test whether and to what extent the quality of democracy increases along with legislatures' oversight capacity and effectiveness. The results of our empirical analyses reveal that while the quality of democracy is related to the effectiveness of oversight and to the fact that a country is democratic (at least formally if not substantively), oversight capacity is not as important as previous studies (Pelizzo, 2008) had suggested. The quality of democracy and the probability that a country is a formal democracy or a liberal democracy are not affected by the number of oversight tools available to the legislature.

Furthermore, our analyses also reveal that, contrary to what international organisations and bilateral agencies had initially believed (USAID, 2000), effectiveness of oversight is not a function of oversight capacity. We conclude by arguing that this evidence should induce international organisations and bilateral agencies to modify their democracy and development promotion strategies. What they need to promote is effective oversight, not simply oversight capacity.

Section one: democracy, democratisation and democratic quality

The literature on democracy can, broadly speaking, be divided into three streams: one devoted to exploring the question of what is democracy, one devoted to the study of the conditions that facilitate the transition from non-democratic rule to democratic rule and one devoted to the study of what makes democracy survive.[2] In this respect, scholars have emphasised the importance of political culture, political institutions, socio-economic development and above all legitimacy.[3]

Various streams of research have in fact suggested that democracy can survive only in countries that provide for cultural, institutional and socio-economic conditions, a favourable setting for the survival of democracy. We will briefly assess the key points of each of these analytical frameworks.

Political Culture

Some scholars have underlined the importance of political culture. For Lipset (1959), the survival of democracy was in large measure due to whether the elites and the masses had pro-democratic values, that is, whether they thought that democracy was the best political regime. For Almond and Verba (1963), the consolidation of democracy had to do with the presence/absence of a civic culture. They suggested that countries that were tolerant of diversity, rational, pragmatic, that believed in the power of persuasion and moderation, and where decisions were made with good sense and were accepted in a fairly consensual manner, were more likely to be a receptive soil for democratic ideas and culture than those countries where such conditions were not satisfied. While an important body of research has underlined the importance of political culture and values in making democracy work (Putnam, 1993), in the course of the past few decades democracy has become consolidated even in countries that were not known for their democratic culture. For example, southern European democracies (Italy, Portugal and Spain) and Latin American democracies, where a majority of the population is Catholic (and therefore believed to have conservative and possibly pro-authoritarian values [Lipset, 1959]), have emerged and have consolidated.

Form of government

Other scholars have instead emphasised that the consolidation and the survival of democracy depend on a country's constitutional design. In this respect, the most famous argument, advanced by Juan Linz (1994), is that the presidential form of government is less likely to sustain democracy because it is characterised by dual legitimacy and rigidity as the executive and the legislative branches are both directly elected for a fixed term in office. Presidential systems' ability to sustain democracy is particularly low when the party system is highly fragmented (Mainwaring, 1993).

Party system attributes

Party systems scholars, such as Sartori (1976), have suggested instead that the stability of democratic regimes and their ability to consolidate and survive depends on the characteristics of the party system. In fact, building on the work of Lowell (1897), Finer (1932) and Hermens (1941), Sartori went on to show that highly fragmented and ideologically polarised party systems make it impossible for governments to function, government performance is thus undermined, the political system does not have any performance-based legitimacy and ultimately collapses. Sartori (1976) showed that the constitutional order of all those countries where the party system was highly fragmented and polarised collapsed. Sartori, in the same vein as Lipset and Rokkan (1967) or Duverger (1954), believed that the fragmentation of the party system was the product of institutional features, such as the electoral system and the country's cleavage structure, while ideological polarisation was the product of the number and the depth of political cleavages. More recent work (Pelizzo and Babones, 2007) has shown instead that the ideological polarisation of a party system is not simply the product of structural conditions such as the cleavage structure, the segmentation of society and so on, but that it is also a function of economic conditions. Specifically, they showed that as economic conditions worsen, in highly fragmented party systems, the distribution of votes becomes more polarised, the government parties become weaker and unable to sustain effective government and thus run in exactly the kind of problems that Sartori (1976) had theorised.

Ethnic diversity

Sartori and the other party system scholars thought that the fragmentation and ideological polarisation of the party system could undermine the stability of government and legislatures but could eventually create the conditions for a democratic breakdown. More recent studies have indicated that party system attributes (fragmentation and polarisation) are a proximate cause of poor democratic governance, but they are not the ultimate cause. For example, Reilly (2006) argued that ethnic diversity or fragmentation is what prevents parties from becoming properly institutionalised, the party system from becoming properly consolidated and democracy from working well and possibly surviving.

Democracy and development

A very large body of research, sparked by the publication of Lipset (1959), has argued that the single most important determinant of democratic consolidation is represented by a country's level of development. Development was believed to create the conditions for the survival of democracy for three basic reasons. First, development contributed to the survival of democracy because in developed societies citizens are more educated and have pro-democratic values. Second, development stabilised democracies because in developed societies there are more resources that can be allocated among competing social groups and the redistribution of resources plays a key role in neutralising conflicts. Finally, development contributed to the survival of democracy because economic success provides the democratic regime with performance-based legitimacy that is so important to make democracy survive. Moreover, scholars noted that democracies were more developed than non-democratic regimes and hypothesised that democracy created the conditions for development, which, in its turn, was crucial for the survival of democracy.[4]

Legitimacy and the quality of democracy

Some of the previous studies suggested that democratic consolidation could be signalled by whether democracy had survived three electoral cycles, whether there had been at least two pacific transfers of executive power, whether democracy had survived at least 20 or 25 years. Now, however, the most widely accepted view is that democratic consolidation is indicated by legitimacy, that is, by "the capacity of a political system to engender and maintain the belief that existing political institutions are the most appropriate or proper ones for society" (Lipset, 1959).

Morlino (1986) developed a more nuanced notion of what is democratic consolidation. For Morlino, democratic consolidation involves not only an increasing legitimacy of the democratic norms and procedures but also the institutionalisation (Huntington, 1968; Panebianco, 1983) of democratic processes and procedures. In this instance, institutionalisation determines the primary characteristics of the democratic system, while at the same time it allows the secondary characteristics of the system to adapt to changing circumstances.

In short, most of Morlino's (1986) theoretical work has addressed the question of how the legitimacy/democratic compromise can be preserved. Lipset (1959) regarded legitimacy as an affective/emotional attachment to a political system for what might be called "cultural" reasons. Thus, for example, the culture of the Junkers in the wake of World War I was not pro-democratic and this contributed to to the failure of the Weimar republic. Lipset rejected the notion that legitimacy could be performance-based and went on to argue that, had the Weimar republic enjoyed some legitimacy, it would have been able to survive the economic catastrophe of the 1920s. Huntington (1991) noted instead that legitimacy can come in many guises, one of which is performance-based, and he argued that while democratic regimes have some procedural legitimacy that non-democratic regimes lack, they are also prone to collapse if they are unable to tackle major economic crises. Morlino, in his work, has adopted a different focus and has suggested that democratic consolidation involves two distinct processes.

According to Morlino, the first process concerns whether the legitimacy that democracy enjoys in a given country is exclusive or inclusive. Legitimacy is said to be exclusive when some important segments of the socio-economic elites "do not accept democratic institutions" while it is said to be inclusive when "all the political organisations are integrated and involved in the acceptance and the support of democratic institutions" (Morlino, 2001: 227). For Morlino, a democratic system that has a high level of legitimacy is consolidated, stable and is good or, to put things in a slightly different way, has a good democratic quality.

Morlino and the quality of democracy

Building on his previous work on democratic transitions and consolidation, Morlino's (2005) most recent inquiries have attempted to further our understanding of the quality of democracy. In his most recent contributions to the study of the quality of democracy, Morlino (2005) made several related claims: that good democracies are political regimes that have a high democratic quality and that the notion of democratic quality can be used to describe/assess: (i) the procedures adopted by a democratic regime; (ii) the characteristics of the democratic regime (output); and (iii) legitimacy of the political regime (outcome) that is its ability to preserve the conditions for its own survival and becoming self-sustaining.

Morlino's (2005) framework for the analysis of the quality of democracy further argues that democracies' performance and quality in terms of procedures, content (output) and result (outcome) can be assessed on the basis of eight sub-components, grouped under three dimensions. They are: (i) the rule of law, electoral accountability, inter-institutional accountability along with the level of participation and the level of political competition – which pertain to the *procedural* sphere; (ii) the freedom and the equality of the social construct all represent the *structural* characteristics or the content of the democratic regime under consideration (*output*); and (iii) the *responsiveness* of the political regime and ultimately its legitimacy – which concern the political regime's ability to address voter demands and create the conditions for a self-sustaining democratic rule (*outcome*). Table 4.1 provides a summary of this framework for analysis: it shows that the quality of democracy concerns these three different dimensions (procedure, content, result) and their eight sub-components.

According to Morlino (2005), the first set of democratic sub-dimensions concerns the procedural aspects of democracy. By focusing on this set of sub-dimensions we can see that some of them

Table 4.1 Determinants of democratic quality

		Rule of law
	Procedures	Electoral accountability
		Inter-institutional accountability
		Participation
		Competition
Democratic quality	Content (outputs)	Freedom
		Equality
	Result (outcomes)	Responsiveness /legitimacy

pertain to the representative aspect of democracy, while others pertain to the way decisions are made in a democratic system. Specifically, competition, participation and electoral accountability pertain to what could be regarded as the representative dimension of democracy. Without multi-party competition, high levels of voter participation and voters' ability to access free information regarding the electoral campaign and to determine the outcome of the electoral competition, elections fail to perform their basic democratic/representative function. Alternatively, the rule of law, the absence of corruption (and other forms of unethical behavior) and inter-institutional accountability pertain to what could be regarded as the *decisional* dimension of democracy.

Morlino' second dimension concerns the content of a democratic regime, namely its ability to promote both *freedom* and *equality*. These are viewed in Morlino's framework as the *output* of democratic decisions.

Morlino's third dimension relates to the ability of a democratic regime to be *responsive* to the electorate, that is, to satisfy the electorate's present demands and/or to anticipate the electorate's future demands.

This multi-dimensional framework is useful not only to identify and assess the qualities of democracy cross-nationally but also to categorise democratic regimes. Countries where all these qualities are lacking are non-democracies, countries were all these qualities are present are perfect democracies, while the in-between cases should be regarded as imperfect, egalitarian and effective democracies depending on the combination of democratic qualities.

Specifically, for Morlino (2005) *effective* democracies are regimes characterised by the presence of the rule of law; *responsible* democracies are those that in addition to the rule of law also display

Rule of law	Accountabilities	Responsiveness	Freedom	Equality	Outcome
+					Effective
+	+				Responsible
+	+	+			Legitimate
+	+		+		Free
+	+			+	Egalitarian
+	+	+	+	+	Perfect

Figure 4.1 Democratic qualities and types of democracies

significant levels of accountability; *legitimate* democracies are those where in addition to the previous two qualities there is also responsiveness; *free* democracies have in addition to the previous three qualities, significant levels of freedom; *egalitarian* democracies in addition to rule of law, accountability and responsiveness have equality; whereas *perfect democracies* score highly in each of these five dimensions – (see figure 4.1.)[5]

Morlino's framework has been used to assess the qualities of democracy, to empirically investigate the connectedness among such democratic qualities, and to develop a better taxonomy of democratic regimes. But more importantly, for the purposes of this book, the framework designed by Morlino explains quite clearly why legislative oversight may be relevant to promote or improve the overall quality of a democratic regime. In fact,

if the overall quality of a democratic regime is a function of how well it fares in terms of functioning, output and outcome;
if the functioning of a democratic regime is a function of the level of inter-institutional accountability; and
if the level of inter-institutional accountability is, to some extent, a function of legislative oversight;
then the overall quality of a democratic regime is a function, among other things, of legislative oversight.

This line of reasoning can be formulated as a causal chain:

Legislative oversight – > inter-institutional accountability – > good functioning of the democratic system – > high quality of democracy.

While Morlino (2005) provided a theoretical justification for why legislative oversight and the quality of democracy may be related to one another, empirical studies conducted by international organisations (e.g. Pelizzo and Stapenhurst, 2008) tested whether the quality of democracy and legislative oversight were empirically related to one another. Specifically, these studies performed two sets of analyses: first, they investigated whether the quality of democracy was higher in countries where the legislature was better equipped to oversee government activities; second, they investigated whether the probability that a political regime was at least a formal democracy and the probability that a political regime was at least a liberal democracy was a function of the legislature's ability to oversee the executive branch. This kind of analysis was conducted under the assumption that the quality of democracy is a function of effective oversight and of the assumption that the effectiveness of oversight activities was simply a function of the number of oversight tools at the disposal of a legislature. In the rest of this chapter, we plan to show whether and to what extent these earlier studies were correct in making such assumptions and whether the quality of democracy is indeed related to oversight (effective, real or potential).

Section two: testing the cases

In the course of the past decade, international organisations devoted to either the promotion of democracy or socio-economic development, regarded legislative strengthening programs as integral parts of their democracy/development promotion programmes. The line of reasoning that was followed by both sets of organisations was that stronger legislatures, that is, legislatures with greater oversight capacity, would be able to perform more effectively their oversight function and keep governments accountable for their actions and could prevent governments from engaging in activities that could be detrimental to either democracy or development. The theoretical framework developed by Morlino (2005) allows us to formulate a theoretical justification for why legislatures with greater oversight capacity are good for democracy.

By stating that democracy and its quality pertain to three different spheres, and that these spheres are inherently multi-dimensional, it becomes apparent that it is theoretically inappropriate for a scholar working within Morlino's framework to argue that greater oversight capacity is good for democracy *tout court*. Rather, the argument should be that by strengthening legislatures' oversight capacity, legislatures are enabled to perform their oversight function more effectively and in so doing they keep the government accountable. In other words, greater oversight capacity contributes to the procedural dimension of democratic quality by ensuring what Morlino regards as one of the essential procedural aspects of a democratic regime, that is, inter-institutional accountability.

It is possible to hypothesise that legislatures with greater oversight capacity can be more effective in keeping governments accountable and thereby securing the rule of law and/or preventing corruption, as we will test in the next chapter. One could also argue that by ensuring government accountability, stronger legislatures also create the conditions for greater government responsiveness, but where stronger legislatures might be expected to make the greatest difference is in terms of securing inter-institutional accountability.

If we were to properly test this causal argument, it would be necessary to test whether changes in oversight capacity (measured in terms of the number of oversight tools available to the legislature) are conducive to changes in the effectiveness of oversight activity. We could then test whether changes in oversight capacity and effectiveness are conducive to changes in democratic quality. To perform this type of analysis, we would need to have diachronic data that are not actually available. In fact, the only data on oversight capacity that have been collected by WBI in collaboration with IPU are synchronic. The data provide a picture of the number of the type of oversight tools available to a certain number of legislatures in 2001 and in 2009, but they do not provide any diachronic information as to how the number of oversight tools available to a legislature has changed over time.

As a result, we test whether in countries where the legislative oversight capacity is greater, oversight is more effective and the quality of democracy is higher. In the course of the analysis, we use the data on oversight tools that were collected by the 2009 WBI-IPU survey as a proxy of oversight capacity. We use the data on executive constraints provided by Polity IV as a proxy of oversight effectiveness/ inter-institutional accountability and we measure the quality of democracy on the basis of the Gastil index data generated by Freedom House.[6]

When we correlate the Gastil index for the 97 countries that participated in the 2009 WBI-IPU survey (with the number of oversight

Table 4.2 Correlation analysis (sig.)

	Quality of democracy
Number of oversight tools	−.150(.143)
Executive Constraints	−.731**(.000)

tools) and the Polity IV data on executive constraints, we find that both correlation coefficients are negative, which means that countries with higher democratic quality are also characterised by the presence of a larger number of oversight tools and more effective oversight. The data presented in table 4.2 make clear, however, that while the coefficient is negative, strong and statistically significant for the correlation between oversight effectiveness and quality of democracy, the coefficient is not significant for the correlation between quality of democracy and oversight capacity.

Previous analyses (Pelizzo and Stapenhurst, 2004; Pelizzo and Stapenhurst, 2006; Pelizzo and Stapenhurst, 2008; Pelizzo, 2008), performed with the data collected by WBI and IPU in 2001, showed that the probability that a country was at least formally democratic or that it was a proper liberal democracy increased as a function of the oversight capacity of the legislature. These and other studies reached the conclusion that greater oversight capacity is thus good for democracy (and its quality) and that this must have been the case because, it was suggested, greater oversight capacity must have increased oversight effectiveness and, ultimately, inter-institutional accountability.

Those earlier studies, based on the WBI-IPU 2001 survey results, were performed with smaller samples than the one that is now at our disposal. The first of these (Pelizzo and Stapenhurst 2006) was conducted by using only the information generated by 49 legislatures that provided complete information in response to the survey. The second study (Pelizzo, 2008) was conducted by using the information provided by all the 83 legislatures that participated in the survey regardless of whether the legislatures had provided the survey administrators with complete information.

Since those early studies used logit regression models to test whether and to what extent the probability that a country was democratic was a function of the number oversight tools at its disposal, we also perform logit regression analyses in this chapter so that our results may be easily compared to those presented in previous studies.

With regard to formal democracy, when we run the logit model with only one predictor, we find that the number of oversight tools, executive constraints and income level all have a positive and statistically significant impact on the probability that a country is democratic (models 1 to 6). However, when we control for the impact of either executive constraints or income level (models 4 and 5), while the regression coefficient for executive constraints and income level remain strong, positive and significant, the regression coefficients for the number of oversight tools become insignificant. When we assess the impact of oversight capacity on the probability that a country is formally democratic by controlling for the effects of both income level and executive constraints, we find that only the regression coefficient for executive constraints remains statistically significant while the other regression coefficients, while remaining positive, become statistically insignificant.

With regard to liberal democracy, when we run the logit model with only one predictor, we find that while both income level and executive constraints have a strong, positive and statistically significant impact on the probability that a country is liberal democratic, the regression coefficient for the number of oversight tools is not significant (models 1 to 3). Furthermore, when we regress a country's liberal democratic status against either the income level or the executive constraints while controlling for the number of oversight tools, we find that the regression coefficients for income level and executive constraints are statistically significant, while the regression coefficients for the number of oversight tools is never significant. Finally, once we assess the impact of oversight capacity on the probability that a country is liberal democratic by controlling for the effects of both income level and executive constraints, we find that the regression coefficients for executive constraints and income level remain statistically significant while the regression coefficient for oversight capacity is statistically insignificant.

The regression coefficients presented in tables 4.3 and 4.4 suggest several considerations. First of all, they show that the probability that a country is formally democratic or liberal democratic is not affected by the oversight capacity of the legislature – a result that contradicts the findings presented in previous studies. Second, the regression coefficients make it clear that while income levels affect the democratic status of a country, they make it quite clear that income levels are a more important determinant of whether a country is liberal democratic than of whether a country is formally democratic. Third, they show that effective oversight is a key determinant of a country's democratic status as it increases the probability that a country is a formal or a liberal democracy.

These conclusions have significant consequences with regard to the beliefs held by international organisations. International organisations devoted to either democracy promotion or socio-economic development believed that effective oversight was essential for keeping government accountable, minimising corruption, promoting good governance and making democracy work. Legislatures were believed, through the effective performance of their oversight activities, to be able to pacify post-conflict societies (O'Brien, Stapenhurst, Johnston, 2008), curb corruption (Stapenhurst, Johnston and Pelizzo, 2006), reduce poverty (Stapenhurst and Pelizzo, 2002) and secure, along with sustainable growth, economic development.

International organisations also held the belief that legislature's ability to perform their oversight activities effectively and effective oversight were simply a function of the oversight capacity at the disposal of the legislature. In other words, one had simply to expand the range of oversight tools available to a legislature in order to increase its oversight capacity, its ability to oversee the executive, the effectiveness of oversight, the quality of democracy and the level of good governance. Not surprisingly, international organisations and practitioners produced a fairly large body of work on how legislatures' oversight capacity could actually be enhanced. Some studies presented the various approaches to legislative strengthening (Hubli and Schmidt, 2007), others underlined that legislative strengthening was tantamount to securing accountability (Johnston and von Trapp, 2008), or proposed new ways of estimating legislative performance and provided guidelines on how legislatures could actually be strengthened (Johnson and Nakamura, 2006; USAID, 2000).

The results presented in tables 4.3 and 4.4 tell a different story. While they sustain the claim that effective oversight is important for keeping governments accountable and that in turn affects the level or the quality of a democratic system, the results show that oversight *potential*, once we control for the effectiveness of oversight, has very little independent effect on democracy.

One reason why we may find that oversight capacity has no impact on the level of democracy or the probability that a country is a formal/liberal democracy is that the influence of oversight capacity is

Table 4.3 Logit regressions (sig.). Formal democracy, income level and oversight

Model	Logit	Constant	Number of oversight tools	Executive constraints	Income level
1	Formal democracy	−. 284 (.797)	.395 (.045)		
2	Formal democracy	−1.520 (.065)		.785 (.000)	
3	Formal democracy	−.067 (.924)			.865 (.000)
4	Formal democracy	−2.388 (.082)	.163 (.422)	.765 (.000)	
5	Formal democracy	−2.099 (.113)	.356 (.071)		.858 (.008)
6	Formal democracy	−3.443 (.031)	.183 (.356)	.743 (.002)	.505 (.168)

mediated by the role played by effective oversight. Once we control for the effects of the latter, we find little evidence of the effects of the former. We can test this proposition to see whether, from a statistical point of view, the *effectiveness* of oversight is a function of a legislature oversight *capacity*.

By correlating oversight capacity with executive constraints, we find that the correlation coefficient is positive but not significant ($r = .152$) and by regressing executive constraints against oversight capacity we find not only that the regression coefficients are weak and statistically

Table 4.4 Logit regressions (sig.). Liberal democracy, income level and oversight

Model	Logit	Constant	Number of oversight tools	Executive constraints	Income level
1	Liberal democracy	−.327 (.661)	.137 (.330)		
2	Liberal democracy	−5.659 (.000)		1.065 (.000)	
3	Liberal democracy	−3.332 (.000)			1.444 (.000)
4	Liberal democracy	−6.768 (.002)	.178 (.481)	1.068 (.000)	
5	Liberal democracy	−4.757 (.001)	.225 (.242)		1.471 (.000)
6	Liberal democracy	−8.973 (.000)	.274 (.351)	.838 (.000)	1.192 (.001)

insignificant, but we also find that oversight capacity explains a meagre 2.3 per cent in the variance of oversight effectiveness.[7]

This last finding challenges one of the key assumptions or one of the key beliefs of what has been the neo-developmental creed of the past decade. Democracy, and possibly good governance, is affected by *effective* oversight, but strengthening the oversight *capacity* is not how oversight effectiveness can actually be boosted. The fact that some legislatures have more oversight tools at their disposal tells very little as to whether they actually employ these tools and tells us even less as to whether these oversight tools are used effectively.

This set of findings forces international organisations to reconsider their strategy. The question that international organisations should address is no longer how can a legislature oversight capacity be enhanced, that is, how many oversight tools should be made available to a legislature, but rather, how can one ensure that legislatures use the oversight tools at their disposal and use them *effectively*?

Conclusions

One of the key beliefs held by international organisations is that the strengthening of legislatures (the strengthening of their oversight capacity) makes legislative oversight of the executive branch more effective, ensures that government is kept accountable, and this contributes to both the improvement of the democratic quality and to the prevention of corruption and malpractice.

While in the next chapter we investigate whether and to what extent oversight capacity and effective oversight have an impact on a country's level of good governance, corruption and development as the international organisations devoted to the promotion of development and the alleviation of poverty have assumed in the past decade, in this chapter we investigated the relationship between democracy and oversight.

In doing so, we have noted that the idea that legislative oversight may be instrumental in keeping government accountable and ensuring that kind of inter-institutional accountability that is an integral component of the quality of democracy in procedural terms, is consistent with some of the most recent work that scholars have conducted on the quality of democracy.

Specifically, we have noted that the theoretical framework devised by Morlino (2005) posits that the quality of democracy is a multi-dimensional phenomenon that pertains to three distinct spheres—the democratic procedures, the democratic outcomes and the democratic results. Morlino (2001, 2005, 2010) in several of his works makes it clear that the procedural notion of the quality of democracy refers to whether and how well a democratic regime secures the rule of law, participation, competition, electoral accountability as well as inter-institutional accountability.

While there is no reason to believe that legislative oversight may influence electoral accountability, participation or competition, international organisations have forcibly argued that legislatures, by keeping governments accountable, play a key role in the preservation of the rule of law, the prevention of corruption and the promotion of good governance practices. More importantly, international organisations have suggested that by acting as voters' agents, legislatures have a major, beneficial impact on the quality of democracy. In other words, the belief held by international organisations that oversight is beneficial not only for good governance but also for democracy can be reconciled with and justified by the political science literature.

Yet, while political scientists argued that effective oversight was instrumental for ensuring inter-institutional accountability, international organisations, by viewing effective oversight as a mere function of oversight capacity, went on to suggest that the expansion of legislatures' oversight capacity would have been by itself sufficient to ensure effective oversight, keep governments accountable and improve the quality of democracy.

The analyses performed in this chapter suggest a rather different conclusion. The results of our statistical analyses sustain the claim that effective oversight and inter-institutional accountability affect, positively or beneficially, the quality of democratic systems, they provide very little support for the fact that effective oversight is a function of oversight capacity and for the fact that the quality of democracy in a given country may be boosted simply by expanding the oversight capacity of a country's legislature.

We believe that this finding may be of interest not only for legislative studies specialists, for constitutional engineers interested in devising institutional/constitutional arrangements that could best serve democracy by enhancing its qualities, but also for practitioners. Our analyses make it clear that the belief that strengthening legislatures is a necessary and sufficient step for promoting democracy is ill-conceived. The issue that practitioners and international organisations need to tackle is not how many oversight tools a legislature has or how many more oversight tools a legislature should be given, but is instead how to secure that legislatures use the tools that are placed at their disposal and use them effectively.

5 Legislative oversight and corruption

Introduction

In Chapter 4, we considered the relationship between legislative oversight and the quality of democracy. In this chapter, we turn to the relationship between legislative oversight and corruption.

This chapter is divided into three parts. In the first part we discuss how the international community came to conceptualise corruption, its causes and consequences. Specifically, we will show that as international organisations came to realise that corruption could be detrimental to socio-economic development and poverty reduction, they started to regard the reduction of corruption as a key element of their development promotion strategies. Furthermore, corruption came to be regarded as a multi-faceted phenomenon that could only be addressed by developing equally multi-faceted anti-corruption strategies, a key component of which was the strengthening of legislatures' oversight capacity. In other words, international organisations, along with their bilateral counterparts, reached the conclusion that legislatures' oversight potential or capacity was essential for ensuring effective oversight, which in turn was regarded as one of the effective ways to minimise corruption. In reviewing the arguments that international organisations advanced on the relationship between legislative oversight and corruption, we point out that this relationship was generally assumed, and was not subjected to rigorous empirical scrutiny. In the second part of this chapter we subject some of the causal claims advanced by international organisations to empirical verification. In doing so we will highlight the relationship between development and corruption; corruption and the *effectiveness* of oversight; oversight *effectiveness* and oversight *capacity*; and oversight *capacity* and corruption.

We show that while some of the assumptions made by international organisations are correct and are corroborated by the empirical analyses, others are not. Specifically, we show that international organisations were correct in positing that presidential systems display a higher level of corruption than parliamentary systems, that countries with higher levels of corruption have, on average, lower levels of development, and that corruption is inversely related to the effectiveness of oversight. We are also able to show that, in contrast to what had been assumed, the *effectiveness* of oversight, is not simply a function of the oversight *potential* or *capacity* of the legislature; in other words, greater oversight capacity does not necessarily translate into greater oversight effectiveness, for reasons that will be more extensively discussed in Chapter 8. In the third section of this chapter, in addition to drawing some conclusions regarding theoretical and practical implications of our findings, we formulate some educated guesses as to why oversight *capacity* or potential, oversight *activity*, and oversight *effectiveness* should not be assumed to be linearly related to one another. It is clear that in the absence of oversight capacity, the legislature is not able to oversee the actions of the executive, and that in the absence of oversight activity, oversight cannot possibly be effective. However, the effectiveness of oversight is not simply a consequence of the amount of oversight activity that a legislature is able to carry out nor of the amount of oversight activities performed. Furthermore, oversight effectiveness does not necessarily reflect the oversight potential or capacity that a legislature has.

Section one: corruption

Not long ago, corruption remained an issue on the margin of international development. Development practitioners avoided the issue because it was considered a matter of a country's internal politics and not an impediment to development. Some academics even claimed that corruption facilitated development by greasing the wheels of a rigid administration (Huntington, 1968; Neff, 1964).[1] The "Washington Consensus", the development paradigm of the early 1990s, made no reference to corruption control or governance in its list of ten key reforms – to the extent that, if considered at all, corruption was thought to be a byproduct of development (Naím, 1994; Kuczynski and Williamson, 2003).

In the mid-1990s, new empirical research reshaped some of the thinking about corruption. New data refuted the "corruption as grease" claim and, instead, showed how corruption engenders more distortions and intrusions in the economy as public officials look for more ways to extract corrupt payments (World Bank, 1997; Kaufmann, 1997). In contrast to earlier arguments, that higher incomes generally lead to better governance, the new research suggested a strong causal effect running the other way: that control of corruption leads to higher income levels (Mauro, 1997) and to such development outcomes as lower infant mortality rates and higher rates of literacy (Kaufmann, 2000). This body of work challenged the notion that governance is a "luxury good" that automatically accrues with wealth accumulation – an assertion often used as a justification for complacency. Instead, the research affirmed that concerted efforts to improve governance and address corruption are required even during periods of robust growth. This research also affirmed the significant negative impact of corruption on economic growth. Mauro's examination of more than a hundred countries offered a quantitative estimate of this effect. He found that if a given country were to improve its corruption score by 2.38 points on a ten-point scale, its annual per capita GDP growth would rise by over half a percentage point (Mauro, 1997).

Corruption can weaken economic growth through many channels. Unsound policies, unpredictable processes and distorted public expenditures resulting from vested interests lead to macro-economic instability, weakened property rights, reduced competition, inefficient allocation of resources, deteriorated physical infrastructure and smaller expenditures on education (Hellman, Jones and Kaufmann, 2000; Tanzi and Davoodi, 1997; Mauro, 1997).

For business, corruption increases risks and uncertainty, entails payments that represent a kind of tax, and requires more management time spent negotiating with public officials. As a result, it dampens investment (Mauro, 1997; Wei and Kaufmann, 1998) and pushes firms into the unofficial economy (Friedman, Johnson, Kaufmann, and Zoido-Lobaton, 2000; and Johnson, Kaufmann, McMillan and Woodruff, 2000). Where corruption provides more lucrative opportunities than productive work, the allocation of talent also deteriorates (Murphy, Shleifer and Vishny, 1991).

At its root, corruption flourishes in conditions of poverty and weak public institutions. Bad incentives and systems, rather than bad ethics, induce people to act corruptly. That is why corruption tends to be more prevalent in developing and transition countries. Poverty creates perverse incentives for public officials, businesspeople and households. For public officials, the motivation to extract corrupt payments is often high as they receive low and sometimes irregular salaries and face significant risks of illness, accidents and unemployment.[2] For businesspeople, the motivation to pursue wealth through corruption is high as scarce capital, poorly skilled workers, a low demand for consumer goods and other conditions decrease the prospects for advancement in the market (Johnston, 1993). For households, the motivation to pay a bribe is high where goods and services are scarce and otherwise may not be available, such as medical services.

More generally, poverty weakens the mechanisms for securing government accountability. Poverty keeps people focused on survival and limits their time and energy to hold leaders to account.[3] Low levels of development also reduce education and literacy, which limits the ability of citizens to serve as watchdogs over officials' activities (Treisman, 2000). Within the government, low levels of development also reduce the resources to implement and maintain monitoring and oversight mechanisms (World Bank, 2000). Research suggests that economic development explains more of the variation in corruption levels across countries than any other variable: in Treisman's cross-country study, for example, per capita income explained between half to three-quarters of the variation in perceived corruption indexes, depending on which set of indexes he used (Treisman, 2000).

Separate from such consequences of poverty, an inadequate framework for government accountability can facilitate corruption. A lack of transparency, inadequate oversight, weak enforcement, and ineffective electoral systems reduce the likelihood of exposure and censure for wrongdoing, and push the cost-benefit calculus in favour of corruption. On the one hand, mechanisms of accountability can operate to greater or lesser effect across different branches and units of government. Such mechanisms of horizontal accountability include anti-corruption legislation, ethics codes, internal reporting and whistle blowing, audit requirements, investigative bodies, prosecutors, the judiciary, law enforcement and legislative oversight. Evidence from a private sector survey finds, for example, that reported levels of corruption are higher where judicial predictability is weak (World Bank, 1997).

On the other hand, vertical mechanisms of accountability operate between government and the public. Such mechanisms of vertical accountability include free and fair elections, competitive political party funding, freedom of information, a free and independent media, and freedom of assembly and speech.

Alongside a weak accountability framework, an unprofessional civil service can facilitate corruption. Abuses of patronage, nepotism and favouritism orient employees toward exchanges of personal favours and compliance with patrons' wishes rather than toward impartial and efficient performance of their jobs. In extreme cases, employees do not have an incentive to perform their official duties, but actually pay for their jobs with the understanding they will make money through bribes. The strongest antidote to this problem is meritocracy in hiring, promoting and firing civil servants, and government surveys confirm that meritocracy has a strong association with corruption control (World Bank, 1997). By contrast, the evidence on civil service pay is often ambiguous. The difference between public and private salaries may represent a "rate of temptation" and have a positive association with corruption, but simply raising public sector salaries may not reduce corruption. Instead, complementary reforms, such as improved accountability, must accompany pay reform to have any effect on corruption.

Another institutional weakness that facilitates corruption is a state's intrusive stance in the economy. Policies that create an artificial gap between demand and supply or that increase public officials' discretion create opportunities for corruption. Such policies include a high degree of state ownership and service provision, excessive business regulation and taxes, arbitrary application of regulations, and trade restrictions. In this context, officials can profit from their office through such corrupt acts as bribes, extortion, asset stripping and selling jobs. Data confirm that corruption is more prevalent in countries with highly distorted policies (World Bank, 1997).

Related to this, an uncompetitive private sector can also fuel corruption. In some transition and developing countries, for example, a source of corruption is the concentration of economic power in monopolies that then wield political influence on the government for private benefits. The problem is particularly acute in natural resource-rich countries, where private monopolies in oil and gas, for example, wield considerable economic and political power that leads to different forms of corruption: non-payment of taxes, off-shore accounts, purchasing licenses and permits, and purchasing votes and decrees that restrict entry and competition. According to Kaufmann (2006), the way to address this kind of corruption is to de-monopolise, deregulate, and facilitate competition. Kaufmann (2006), Johnston and Kpundeh (2001) and others have highlighted the fact that reducing corruption requires tackling these underlying causes. Especially where corruption is widespread, curbing corruption through investigations and enforcement on a case-by-case basis is not enough. The effort also needs to reduce opportunities for corruption, increase competition in the economy, strengthen political accountability, increase civil society participation and improve incentives for good performance. These reforms target the relationships among core state institutions, the interactions between the state and firms, the relationship between the state and civil society, the political system, and public administration.

The nature and importance of public sector management reforms, political accountability, civil society participation and a competitive private sector with regard to curbing corruption have been discussed elsewhere (Kaufmann, 2006). This chapter is concerned with how the *institutional restraints* on power can be an important mechanism in checking corruption. This mechanism of "horizontal" accountability creates checks and balances within the government by separating powers among state institutions. If given adequate independence, the legislative (and judicial) branches can restrain abuses of power by the executive branch and penalise abuses if they occur. Hence legislatures came to represent a key component in the developmental paradigm of horizontal accountability.

This developmental paradigm assumed that legislatures could exercise oversight of the executive through public accounts and audit committees which would require disclosure of government documents and which could implement sanctions. International organisations came to believe in the following set of causal relations: development was negatively affected by corruption, corruption could be minimised through effective oversight, effective oversight was a function of a legislature oversight capacity (number of oversight tools at the disposal of the legislature itself) and, therefore, that by strengthening legislative capacity, that is, by expanding the number of oversight tools that a legislature could use to oversee the executive, one could increase the effectiveness of oversight, minimise corruption and promote development.

While the validity of this set of causal relations has generally been assumed, it has never been subjected to a proper empirical verification – which is what we now undertake.

Section two: oversight, development and corruption

In this section we perform some empirical, that is, statistical, analyses to test whether and to what extent international organisations were correct in assuming that effective oversight reduces corruption, that corruption prevents development and that oversight potential or capacity is responsible for the effectiveness of oversight. Specifically, we want to examine four propositions:

i) whether lower levels of development are to be found in countries where there are higher levels of corruption (and conversely whether higher levels of development can be found in countries that have lower levels of corruption);
ii) whether lower levels of corruption are to be found in countries where oversight activities are carried out more effectively;
iii) whether oversight activities are more effective in countries where legislatures have more oversight tools at their disposal; and
iv) whether lower levels of corruption are to be found in countries where legislatures have greater oversight capacity.

The data employed in the course of this analysis were collected by the World Bank Institute (WBI) and the Inter-Parliamentary Union (IPU) in 2009, which was discussed in some detail in previous chapters. The data on executive constraints, that is, our proxy for the effectiveness of oversight, are taken from Polity IV; the data on development are taken from the World Bank development indicators (WBDI). Specifically, we used the data provided by the WBDI on the income per capita for each of the countries included in our sample to assess whether countries had high income, upper-middle income, lower-middle income or low income: we created a four-point scale such that low-income countries are assigned a score of 1, countries belonging to the lower-middle income are given a score of 2, countries belonging to the upper-middle income receive a score of 3 and upper-income countries receive a score of 4. Finally, we employ Transparency International's Corruption Perception Index (CPI) as a proxy for the level of corruption in a given country.

Table 5.1 Models development, democracy and corruption (sig.)

	Model 1	Model 2	Model 3
Intercept	.852	3.950	1.717
	(.000)	(.000)	(.000)
CPI	.403		.319
	(.000)		(.000)
Gastil index		−.429	−.166
		(.000)	(.003)
R−squared	.625	.436	.663

Corruption and socio-economic development

The data presented in table 5.1 show that the level of socio-economic development of a given country is strongly influenced by the level of corruption in the country (model 1), by the level of democracy (model 2), and that the impact of corruption on the level of development remains strong and statistically significant even when we control for the impact of the level of democracy (model 3). The results of the third model indicate in fact that even when we control for the quality of democracy, which, as we know from model 2, has a major effect on the level of development, the level of corruption remains the strongest predictor of development and the model explains two-thirds in the variance in socio-economic development. In short, this evidence sustains the claim that international organisations were correct in positing that corruption prevents development and that by eliminating/reducing corruption one creates the conditions for socio-economic development.

Since socio-economic development is a function of corruption (or rather the lack thereof) and the quality of democracy, whatever enhances the quality of democracy or prevents corruption indirectly contributes to the promotion of socio-economic development. From the previous chapter we know that while legislative oversight potential, that is, the number of oversight tools available to a legislature, has a rather insignificant influence on the level/quality of democracy, the effectiveness of oversight is a major determinant of the quality of democracy – and therefore, indirectly, it is a major determinant of socio-economic development.

Oversight effectiveness and level of corruption

The question now becomes, Does oversight effectiveness also affect the level of corruption (or the lack thereof) and does it have a second,

Table 5.2 Corruption, oversight and presidentialism (sig.)

	Model 1	Model 2	Model 3	Model 4
Intercept	2.219	2.317	2.902	3.46
	(.002)	(.037)	(.000)	(.003)
Oversight effectiveness	.420	.422	.360	.370
	(.001)	(.001)	(.003)	(.002)
Oversight capacity		−.018		−.100
		(.909)		(.516)
Presidentialism			−1.215	−1.239
			(.015)	(.014)
R−squared	.136	.136	.199	.203

mediated impact, on a country's level of socio-economic development?

In order to see whether this is the case, we regress the level of corruption against the effectiveness of oversight in the four models presented in table 5.2. In the first model, CPI is regressed simply against the effectiveness of oversight, in the second model we regress CPI against effective oversight controlling for the number of oversight tools available to a legislature, in the third model we regress CPI against effective oversight controlling for a form of government dummy that is turned on when the form of government is presidential and is turned off otherwise. We use this model to test a proposition that has been repeatedly advanced in the literature, namely that the levels of corruption found in countries with a presidential form of government are higher than the levels of corruption registered in countries with other forms of government (Lederman *et al.*, 2005; Gerring and Thacker, 2004; Gerring, Thacker and Moreno, 2005). Hence, we use this model to subject this proposition to an empirical verification.

Assuming, as both scholars and practitioners have often argued and assumed, that countries with a presidential form of government display higher levels of corruption (Kunicova and Rose-Ackermann, 2005), one has to understand whether the association between presidentialism and corruption is spurious or whether presidentialism indeed induces corrupt behaviour and thus generates higher levels of corruption.

There are at least three plausible explanations why higher levels of corruption are found in countries with a presidential form of government: cultural, functional and institutional. The cultural explanation posits that countries with a greater cultural propensity to tolerate corruption also have a cultural appreciation for a more charismatic type of leadership and a greater propensity to have a presidential form of government. In other words, it is not presidentialism *per se* that causes corruption but rather it is a culture that is predisposed to both strong men in politics as well as to presidentialism and a toleration of the misallocation of public resources, patrimonialism and corruption and other forms of unethical behaviour. This explanation travels quite well from Latin America to Africa and South East Asia.

The functional explanation of the relationship between presidentialism and corruption is that since the existence of a presidential form of government may endanger the survival of democracy (see Chapter 4), corruption can be viewed as the price that has to be paid for democracy to survive in adverse circumstances.

The institutional explanation holds that since legislatures in presidential systems have fewer tools of oversight at their disposal, they are not able to oversee the actions of the executive as well as those countries which have parliamentary forms of government. In this case, presidentialism does not induce corruption by itself, but it allows corruption to remain unchecked, since legislatures in these systems do not have the tools to keep it under control.

The fourth model presented in table 5.2 allows us to see which of these explanations is supported by the most compelling evidence. The data presented suggest several considerations. First, international organisations were quite right in positing that the effectiveness with which oversight activities are performed affects the level of good governance and contributes to the prevention of corruption, which, as the data presented in table 5.1 have already illustrated, is detrimental to socio-economic development. In fact, the regression coefficient for the effectiveness of oversight remains strong and statistically significant in each of the four models employed here. Second, the data make it clear that the oversight capacity of a legislature has no statistical impact on the level of corruption once we control for the effectiveness of oversight. More importantly, and this is our third finding, the regression coefficients of the third model make it clear that, as some scholars had long assumed, the presidential form of government is detrimental to good governance. Indeed, even when we control for the impact of the effectiveness of oversight on levels of corruption, it is clear that presidentialism has a strong and negative impact on corruption. However, what the results are unable to tell us is whether presidentialism is detrimental to good governance because in presidential systems corruption is a necessary cost for democracy to survive (the functional explanation), because the culture that promotes presidentialism also fosters patrimonialism and corruption (the cultural explanation), or because presidential systems are less equipped to perform oversight than other forms of government (the institutional explanation). We address each of these explanations in reverse order.

The institutional explanation posits that the relationship between presidentialism and corruption is spurious since presidential systems have fewer oversight tools, since oversight tools are needed to perform effective oversight, since effective oversight is a known determinant of (the lack of) corruption, what causes higher levels of corruption in the presidential system is not the presidential form of government but its lack of oversight tools. In order to see whether it is presidentialism or the oversight capacity in presidential systems that creates the conditions for corruption, we assess the impact of presidentialism on levels of corruption controlling not only for the effectiveness of oversight but also for oversight capacity. Once we do so, the impact of oversight capacity on levels of corruption is weak and statistically insignificant. Hence, we can reject the institutional explanation: the impact of presidentialism on levels of corruption is bad even when the impact of oversight capacity is kept constant.

The functional explanation posits that since presidentialism is less likely to make democracy survive (Linz, 1994) – because its rigidity and dual legitimacy makes it unable to function in highly fragmented party systems – presidential systems need to have higher levels of corruption than other forms of government because resources derived from corrupt behaviour are used to prevent tensions from arising and to preserve the democratic compromise. But if this were the case, we should conclude that it is simply a case of a more general law, namely that corruption is the only way to make democracy survive in adverse conditions – in which case, higher levels of corruption should also be detected in fragile democracies with hyper-fragmented party systems, in countries characterised by high ethnic fragmentation, in countries characterised by high levels of cultural/religious polarisation. We should thus find that high levels of corruption are found in both presidential and non-presidential systems – since party system fragmentation, ethnic fragmentation, religious polarisation are orthogonal to presidentialism, and presidentialism by itself could not be used to predict/explain variation in levels of corruption.

We can reinforce this line of argument with some empirical data. If corruption is the price democracy has to pay to survive under adverse conditions and if presidentialism is one of such adverse conditions because it is a form of government characterised by fixed terms in office and dual legitimacy, then a system that has neither fixed terms nor dual legitimacy should not pose a threat to the survival of democracy and should display lower levels of corruption than those registered in countries with a presidential form of government. Yet we know that semi-presidential countries are on average more corrupt than presidential ones. Hence, we reject the functional explanation.

The cultural explanation for why there are higher levels of corruption in presidential systems than in parliamentary ones is that a political culture that appreciates strong and charismatic leaders (whose status seems to be above the law – as the Platonic statesman was supposed to be for promoting the country's well-being) is a political culture that prefers the presidential form of government. Therefore, if this explanation were correct, the political culture that favours presidentialism is willing to tolerate corruption and this is why corruption in presidential systems is higher than in others. Such an explanation would be quite compelling, even in the absence of further empirical corroboration, if it weren't for the fact that what this explanation posits is that the highest levels of corruption should be recorded in presidential systems. Yet we know that this is not the case as the highest levels of corruption are recorded in semi-presidential settings, in countries that do not have a legacy of Spanish colonialism, and with a small percentage of Catholics in the population.

In other words, the results of our analyses suggests that the real question that needs to be addressed is not so much whether and why there are higher levels of corruption in presidential systems than in parliamentary ones, but why the highest levels of corruption are found in countries with the semi-presidential form of government which, according to its most ardent supporters (Sartori, 1994), combines the best of the parliamentary and the presidential worlds.

The question is of some importance for a simple reason. If presidential systems, which are the least equipped to ensure inter-institutional accountability, presented the highest levels of corruption and if parliamentary systems, which are the best equipped to oversee corruption, presented the lowest levels of corruption (Lederman et al., 2005; Gerring and Thacker, 2004, Gerring, Thacker and Moreno, 2005) and if semi-presidential systems displayed in-between levels of corruption, we could safely conclude that corruption is a function of institutional capacity and that institutional capacity is a function of the form of government, and that would be the end of the story. Yet, we know that this is not the case. So why are the highest levels of corruption recorded in countries with a semi-presidential form of government?

This question cannot be answered on institutional grounds, for legislatures in semi-presidential systems are fairly well equipped (in terms of oversight tools) to oversee the government. Nor can it be answered on functional grounds, because semi-presidential systems do not pose the same threat to democracy that is allegedly posed by the rigidity and dual legitimacy of presidential settings. (We have seen, moreover, that this functional argument does not hold up even in the case of presidentialism.) Finally, even the cultural explanation (that could be invoked in the case of presidential systems) does not apply for semi-presidential systems, since a culture that treasures and fosters a cult of the leader and patrimonialism, would not adopt a form of government where the executive power is split between a president and a prime minister.

The answer, as to why the highest levels of corruption are found in countries with a semi-presidential form of government, needs to be found elsewhere. In our view, the answer could be found in a micro-level, demand-side model. We present this in detail in Chapter 7. But before presenting our strategic interaction model and explaining why we believe it is superior to other models and explanations, we need to say a few words as to why the oversight capacity in semi-presidential settings does not translate into effective oversight and into a greater ability to control corruption.

The literature has provided three basic answers as to why this is the case. The first is that the effectiveness of oversight is not a linear function of oversight capacity but depends on the presence/absence of contextual factors, including party cohesion, party institutionalisation and rule of law, among others. In the absence of such contextual factors, oversight is not exercised effectively (Wang, 2005; Stapenhurst, 2010). The problem with this answer is twofold. It is problematic in the first place because it presents a circular explanation (effective oversight is both a cause and consequence of the rule of law), which ultimately amounts to saying that the rule of law is responsible for the rule of law – a finding that while indisputable is hardly informative. This answer is also problematic for a second reason – that while it is able to specify some conditions that may increase the effectiveness of oversight, when that includes party cohesion, party institutionalisation, rule of law, among others, it has very little to say regarding the conditions under which such oversight is performed.

The second answer is that while in general it remains true that stronger legislatures (that is, legislatures with greater oversight capacity), are better equipped to oversee the actions of the executive, the reason why they sometimes fail to do so and, as a result, fail to curb corruption, is that in some countries the legislature, and not the executive, is the most corrupt institution in the country. Practitioners have then suggested that proper legislative strengthening must involve not only the expansion of oversight capacity, without which the executive branch cannot be overseen, but also the adoption of institutional features such as legislative codes of ethics, codes of conduct and ethics committees, designed to prevent legislative corruption. While there is some merit to this line of thinking, this explanation is not fully satisfactory. First, it does not solve a basic behavioural dilemma, namely why should corrupt legislatures (and legislators) adopt and use codes of conduct and other institutional devices designed to eliminate a system in which they (legislators) prosper both individually and collectively. And second, this argument fails to explain why in some settings legislatures have, in spite of how corrupt they are perceived to be, adopted new oversight tools, and enacted ethics reforms.

One could of course minimise the importance of the objections to the second explanation, by saying that pressures from the international community may change the systems of incentives under which politicians operate. Politicians, whose sincere preference would be to preserve corruption, are induced for strategic reasons (such as, for example, to maximise their chances to be re-elected) to launch an anti-corruption campaign that otherwise they would rather avoid. But this explanation is not terribly convincing by itself. While pressures from international organisations may at times be of some importance, they do not provide an adequate explanation for the politics of legislative ethics reforms for several reasons.

First of all, all politics is local. For politicians to be elected, they need to win elections in their districts and constituencies. If they disrupt the system of corruption that provides them with the means to keep their respective voters satisfied, they would not be competitive in the electoral campaign and would thus decrease their chances of being re-elected. Furthermore, by doing what international organisations suggest, reform-minded MPs would be at odds with their respective political parties and this would jeopardise their political careers. In an anti-corruption and legislative strengthening workshop we ran in 2004, one of us contacted a member of a South East Asian legislature, who in the course of the workshop had been extremely vocal in encouraging good governance and reducing corruption. We inquired whether he needed materials and support to run some anti-corruption activities in his home country. He said that he would have loved to run anti-corruption activities in his country, but since he attached greater value to his political career than to good governance, he had no desire to endanger the former to promote the latter.

Second, as international pressures to curb corruption are generally directed towards developing countries, local politicians could (as some scholars would) derubricate international pressures as neo-colonial efforts to interfere with proper functioning of legitimate public officials and offices in sovereign states. Hence, given the local nature of politics, international pressures are not always necessary or able to promote good governance and legislative ethics reforms.

If the presence/absence of contextual factors or the corrupt/honest nature of legislatures are not responsible for the effective performance of oversight activities, then what can account for the effectiveness of oversight? Our explanation, which will be explained further in Chapter 7, is essentially behavioural and begins with the structure of incentives with which politicians are confronted. Specifically, we suggest that whether politicians (even corrupt ones) adopt legislative ethics and good governance reforms depends on whether there is a demand domestically for good governance. If there is no demand, regardless of how dysfunctional a country may be, how corrupt it is or how much international pressure there is to change, reforms will not be adopted. If there is some demand among the electorate for good governance, regardless of whether there is international pressure to promote good governance, politicians feel pressure to adopt some reforms to satisfy voter demands. If voter demand for good governance is satisfied by the adoption of oversight tools, the creation of ombud offices and anti-corruption agencies, then politicians can simply establish these offices for cosmetic reasons without actually empowering them. Alternatively, where voter demands for good governance are not satisfied by mere cosmetic changes, the political system will be forced not only to create/adopt instruments to fight corruption, but also to use them effectively.

In Chapter 7 we will present our model at greater length and support its analytical merit by presenting evidence that we gathered through field work. We suggest that creating a popular demand for good governance is potentially the most relevant strategy international organisations could adopt. In the absence of a local demand for good governance, anti-corruption measures are neither adopted nor enforced – which is precisely why, even when it is available, oversight capacity or potential is not translated into effective oversight.

Conclusions

In this chapter we tested a set of propositions that international organisations have regarded as self-evident truths, namely that corruption is bad for development, that effective oversight curbs corruption, and that effective oversight is a function of oversight capacity.

The analyses performed reveal that there is a clear negative relationship between corruption and development and that this relationship between these two variables remains strong and significant even when we control for the impact of democracy – another important determinant of development. Furthermore, our models show that while more than 60 per cent in the variance in levels of development is explained by levels of perceived corruption alone, about 42 per cent of the variance is explained by levels of democracy and that about 66 per cent of the variance is explained when we regress levels of development against corruption and democracy. The meaning of this finding is clear: corruption is detrimental to development and international organisations have been quite correct in positing that such a relationship existed.

Second, our analysis also makes clear that those countries in which legislative oversight is performed effectively record the lowest levels of corruption. The analysis also indicates that effective oversight is not a function of oversight capacity, and that oversight capacity has virtually no impact – either directly or indirectly – on levels of corruption. Thus, while international organisations were correct in assuming that effective oversight is instrumental in curbing corruption, they were mistaken in assuming that effective oversight could simply be promoted by enhancing legislatures' oversight capacity.

We therefore suggest that international organisations need to understand why oversight tools are actually used or not, why they are used effectively in some instances but not in others, and why the availability of a full set of oversight tools leads to very effective oversight in some countries and not in others. In this chapter, we have formulated an answer that we plan to explain in greater detail in the Chapter 7, and which we will also test against a particular case in Chapter 8. We believe that the basic explanation that we need to seek is micro-level, agency-based and behavioural. Before so doing, however, we examine some of these factors in an in-depth study of legislative oversight in Ghana (in the next chapter).

6   Legislative oversight in Ghana

Introduction

Building on the findings in Chapters 3, 4 and 5, in this chapter we show that while the existence of legislative oversight tools matters in that such tools improve the quality of governance and the legitimacy of the political system, their impact is conditional and it depends on the presence of contextual factors. In this regard, the results support the conclusions of Olson and Norton (1996) and Norton and Ahmed (1999) who claim that contextual factors determine the effectiveness of legislatures and that internal factors, such as oversight tools, are only supportive.

We do so by focusing on the case of the Parliament of Ghana. We are able to show two substantive results: first that as the Parliament of Ghana has become a more pro-active overseer of the executive, that the functioning of the political system has improved and that the legitimacy of the political system has increased; and second that the success of the Ghanaian Parliament was made possible by the effective use of oversight tools at its disposal within a set of specific contextual factors.

The evidence analysed in this chapter comes from two sources. The data on the number and type of oversight tools available to the Parliament of Ghana are taken from the survey conducted by the World Bank Institute (WBI) in collaboration with the Inter-Parliamentary Union (IPU) in 2009. All the other data were collected in the course of field research that we carried out in Ghana. Our research comprised in-country document search, 52 personal interviews (18 with politicians, 16 with parliamentary staff, 9 with civil society representatives and 9 with journalists) and four focus groups (one with each of politicians, parliamentary staff, civil society representatives and journalists), each of which comprised between four and seven participants. The focus groups comprised different participants from the personal interviews. A fifth focus group was conducted with a selection of earlier participants, and preliminary analyses and conclusions were presented and validated.

The chapter is organised in the following way. In the first section, we discuss the context in which the Parliament of Ghana operates. Attention is paid to the constitutional dispositions pertaining to the parliament and executive–legislative relations. In the second part we show that an increase in the amount of oversight activities performed by the Parliament of Ghana has gone hand in hand with an increase in the legitimacy of Ghanaian Parliament and democracy. In the third part we discuss some of the contextual factors that, according to our respondents, created the conditions for the success of the Ghanaian Parliament. In the fourth and final section we will draw some tentative conclusions.

Section one: the Ghanaian political environment

Ghana attained independence from the United Kingdom on 6 March 1957. In the 50 years since independence the country has had four republican regimes in 1960, 1969, 1979 and 1992. The fourth republican regime has been the longest. Under the fourth republic there have been five elections, the first two won by Jerry Rawlings (1992, 1996), the second two by John Kuffour (2000, 2004) and the fifth by John Atta Mills (2008). Between the four republican governments there were coup d'états, followed by military governments, in 1966, 1972, 1978, 1979 and 1981.

Since 1992, Ghana has emerged as one of the few African countries where peaceful change of government has occurred. The most recent election occurred on 7 December, 2008. None of the parties secured the required 50 plus one majority for an outright win. Following a runoff between the ruling New Patriotic Party (NPP) and the National Democratic Congress (NDC), the major opposition party on 28 December, the NDC emerged as the winner. This marks the second alternation of government: in December 2000 power was transferred from the NDC to the NPP and now, back to the NDC.

This period, after 16 years[1] of military rule, coincided with high ratings from Freedom House: from a low of six (not free) in 1991 to a current high of two (free) in political rights and civil liberties.[2]

Similarly, the most recent Afrobarometer surveys, conducted in March 2008, demonstrate that nearly 80 per cent of Ghanaians overwhelmingly prefer democracy over military rule, one-party government, or dictatorship, and 86 per cent of Ghanaians consider elections and the rule of law as the best vehicle for selecting leaders and maintaining order in the society.[3] This evidence shows that the quality of democracy has improved and that the democratic regime has a high level of legitimacy, which, we will show later on is to a considerable extent a function of the improvements in the quality of parliament's oversight activities. Not surprisingly, the Afrobarometer surveys show that Ghanaians consistently recognise parliament as the major institution in a democracy whose supreme responsibility is to check the executive and restrain it from exceeding its constitutional powers.

The 1992 Constitution is the foundation for the country's Fourth Republic (Gyimah-Boadi, 2001); it prescribes a hybrid, or semi-presidential system of government. The president is popularly elected to a four-year term of office, but unlike the pure presidential system of government, the majority of the cabinet members must be Members of Parliament. Under the constitution, the Parliament is the sole law-making branch of government with autonomy over its agenda (Article 93). Parliament can remove the President, Vice President and Speaker (Article 69), but the President cannot dissolve Parliament. The uniqueness of the constitutional design was intended as a "remedy against past failures" (Lindberg and Zhou, 2009).

The Parliament of Ghana is a unicameral legislature, with 230 members who must be appointed to at least one but no more than three standing committees; there are 14 Standing Committees and 19 Select Committees.[4] Parliament has fairly extensive oversight powers or capacity as revealed in a recent survey conducted by IPU and WBI.[5] The responses provided by the Parliament of Ghana indicated that the government is collectively responsible to Parliament, as required by the Constitution and several acts of Parliament, that the Parliament can keep the government accountable by lodging motions of censure, by taking votes on governments' reports, and in ultima ratio by impeaching the government for its actions, as we will shortly discuss.

In fact, in addition to the dispositions established by the articles 53, 54 and 76–80 of the Standing Orders and that concern other types of motions, articles 104–7 of the Standing Orders enable the Parliament to introduce a resolution/motion for the removal of the President and the Vice President as well as for a Vote of Censure against a Minister. The motion for the censure on a minister has to be introduced by at least one-third of the MPs and has to be approved by at least a two-thirds majority. The same requirements apply also for tabling and approving a motion for the removal of the President and the Vice President.

However, in responding to the survey questionnaire, the Ghanaian respondent indicated that no motion of censure had been adopted in the last ten years. There are two possible explanations for the inability of Parliament to censor any Minister. First, under the hybrid system in Ghana, the President is required by the constitution to nominate ministers from parliament. Strategically, the President usually co-opts active MPs by nominating them for ministerial assignments. Apart from inducing them to switch their allegiance from the legislature to the executive, the selection of the effective MPs denies parliament some of its best legislators. Besides, MPs have over the years built very strong collegial relationships prior to and in parliament. Without doubt, these informal relationships tend to trump the formal institutional infrastructure ushered in by the constitution. Previous research demonstrates that constitutional powers are insufficient in determining the powers of the legislature (Patzelt, 1994; Norton, 1998) because of the incongruity between formal and actual powers (Wang, 2005). Formal definitions (de jure) do not always translate into practice. Formal institutions in Africa lack effective authority because of deeply personalised authority (Chabal and Daloz, 1999) which tends to supersede formal authority. In addition, the tendency to override formal institutions has been enabled by a weak legal system (Bratton, 2007).

The second reason for parliament's inability to censor ministers is that Ghana has so far experienced a unified government (in contrast to a divided government) in which both the executive and legislature is controlled by the same party. The allegiance of ministers is to the executive and not to parliament. As a result, members of the majority party led by the Speaker of the House are reluctant to embarrass the government and by extension their party whose patronage is essential for MPs to continue to contest elections and hold their seats. The election of MPs in Ghana is party-centred. Consequently, party cohesion and party discipline are very strong. Taken together, party cohesion and discipline ensures predictable voting outcomes (Wehner,

2005) thus diminishing the government's willingness to compromise and negotiate with the minority.[6]

Since international organisations have long believed in the importance of legislative oversight for keeping governments accountable, minimising corruption, promoting good governance, improving the quality of democracy, facilitating democracy's consolidation and the pacification of post-conflict societies, one of the main focuses of the surveys conducted by WBI in collaboration with IPU concerns the tools of legislative oversight.

According to the evidence generated by the WBI-IPU survey, the Parliament of Ghana has at its disposal the following oversight tools: oral and written questions, motions for debate, hearings in committee and the institution of inquiry committees.[7] The respondents indicated that the deadline for replies to oral and written questions is 14 days, that there is some time set aside for questions in the plenary sessions – roughly less than 5 hours per week for less than 32 weeks a year.

If we take the deadline for answering parliamentary questions as an indication of the effectiveness of parliamentary questions as oversight tools, we find that the parliamentary questions in Ghana have more bite than in some African settings but less bite than in others. If we take, for example, the deadline for answering written questions, we can see that the deadline set in Ghana is more stringent than the deadlines established in Benin, Burkina Faso, Burundi, Côte d'Ivoire (Ivory Coast), Gabon, Senegal and Togo, it is as stringent as it is in Cameroon and Uganda and is considerably less stringent than in Kenya and Namibia.[8]

Government members and senior officials may be summoned by committees and may have to participate in the committee work at the request of the committee and the parliament plays a key role in confirming the appointment chairmen of state institutions, heads of independent authorities, ministers, deputy ministers and supreme court judges. Articles 152 and 169 of the Standing Orders of the Parliament of Ghana establish that one of the 14 standing committees of the Parliament of Ghana is the Appointment Committee. This committee, "composed of the First Deputy Speaker as Chairman and not more than other twenty-six members" (art. 169 [1]) has the duty to make recommendations to parliament for approval or rejection with regard to all the presidential nominations for "appointment as Ministers of State, Deputy Ministers, and such other persons as are specified under the Constitution or under any other enactment" (art. 169 [2] [a]) as well as "for appointments as Chief Justice or other Justices of the Supreme Court" (art. 169 [2] [b]).[9] The Appointments Committee is mandated to report to parliament within three days after the conclusion of its deliberation and the parliament takes a vote, by secret ballot, to confirm or reject the presidential nominations for appointment.

In addition to internal tools of legislative oversight, Ghana also has additional oversight bodies such as the Ombudsman (whose functions, we are told by the respondents, are performed by a body called the Commission of Human Rights and Administrative Justice), an anti-corruption agency that reports directly to parliament, and a Supreme Audit Institution (the Auditor General) that also must report to parliament "anytime a report is ready".[10]

Section two: parliament oversight activity and legitimacy

While knowing how many oversight tools are available to a legislature provides an indication of that legislature's oversight potential (Pelizzo and Stapenhurst, 2004; Sartori, 1987) or capacity, it does not provide any information as to whether, how much, how frequently and how effectively those tools are actually used.[11] For example, we know that in spite of the constitutional power to censure a minister, the Parliament of Ghana has never approved a censure, with the exception of one reported futile attempt to do so, on a minister so much so that in the second Parliament of the 4th Republic there were questions about parliament's real ability to censure ministers. But questions emerged also as to what was the parliament's real ability to questions ministers, for it was felt that ministers only appear before the House to respond to routine questions about administrative lapses and bureaucratic delays but they are never seriously challenged and scrutinised for their actions and, more importantly, for the actions of their departments.

The data that we have collected show that in addition to the doubts one may have as to what is the parliament's capacity to question and censure Ministers of State, there are several activities that the parliament performs rarely and with little enthusiasm. The data on the oversight activities performed by the Parliament of Ghana presented in table 6.1 show, for example, that it is rather uncommon, because of constitutional disposition and partisan constraints (as indicated by the extremely high level of cohesion in the

Table 6.1 Frequency with which certain tasks are performed by the parliament

Survey question number	Survey question	Mean score	Std.dev.
1	How frequently does the legislature review appointments	3.5	1.7
2	How frequently does the legislature censure ministers/the president	1.7	0.8
9	How strong is majority (governing) political party cohesion	4.7	0.8

(Yes = 0; No = 1) (Scale of 1–5, where 1 = very weak and 5 = very effective)

governing party), for the parliament to amend the budget, over-ride a presidential veto and censure a cabinet minister.

The data made, however, quite clear that there are also some activities that the parliament performs with much greater frequency and enthusiasm. For example, the parliament has been fairly active in reviewing appointments.

A second area in which parliament has been fairly active is the oversight of the expenditure of public money. The evidence that we collected in the course of the field work suggests that parliamentary committees devoted to this kind of oversight activity have become increasingly active and are believed to be increasingly effective. Oversight committees meet regularly (at least seven times a session), more than they once did (more than 12 times a year), have more bite and make more of a difference.[12] An important development in the last parliament was the opening up of Public Accounts Committee (PAC) hearings to the media and the public.[13] With the support of the Parliamentary Centre, and with the widely acknowledged (by survey respondents) leadership by former Chair, Hon. Samuel Sallas Mensah, PAC hearings were both opened to the public and held in different regions of the country – factors which respondents told us contributed significantly to the effectiveness of the committee. In a now famous case emerging out of its first public hearing in October 2007, the PAC ordered the Ministry of Tourism and two advertising agencies to refund 53 million Ghana cedis and 2,500 US dollars to the government including interest accruing on the amounts.[14] The PAC sitting was prompted by an Auditor General report which revealed financial discrepancies in the accounts of the Ministry of Tourism since 2003. At the public hearing, the PAC members concluded that the

Minister of Tourism and the Chief Director of the Ministry were unable to satisfy the committee about the disbursement of funds allegedly paid for advertisements.[15] In a November 2008 news conference, the Chairman of the PAC reported that the committee has so far recovered $40 million.[16] More generally, respondents also noted a longer-term trend of increased PAC effectiveness: said one, "There has been a dramatic change for the better; in 1993/6 there were no testimonies given to the committee, since 1997 there have been."

Unsurprisingly, given the greater level of activism of parliament and parliamentary committees in the exercise of the oversight function, respondents generally rated the oversight committees as fairly effective in uncovering incidents of fraud and corruption (see table 6.2), with a mean score of 3.2 on a scale of 1–5, where 1 = very ineffective and 5 = very effective. Interestingly, journalists reported

Table 6.2 Tools and mechanisms influencing legislative oversight

Survey question number	Survey question	Mean score	Stddev.
3[17]	Does the legislature amend the budget	0.317	0.5
6[18]	Has the legislature ever over-ridden a presidential veto of legislation	0.118	0.3
12	How effective is the auditor general in uncovering incidents of fraud and corruption	4.2	0.9
	How effective is the ombudsman (chraj) in uncovering incidents of fraud and corruption	3.6	
14	How effective is the anti-corruption agency (sfo) in uncovering incidents of fraud and corruption	3.5	1.3
18	How effective are oversight committees in uncovering incidents of fraud and corruption	3.2	1.5
	How effective are special committees/ commissions of inquiry in uncovering incidents of fraud and corruption	3.8	1.3
16	What is the degree of partisanship within legislative oversight committees	2.2	1.6
	How effective is question period in uncovering incidents of fraud and corruption	3.7	

(Per cent of respondents, n = 1197)

somewhat more success (mean of 3.8) than the MPs themselves (mean 3.3) or parliamentary staff (mean of 3.2) but civil society representatives reported significantly less (mean of 2.4). One senior Member of the PAC commented, however, that " ... the PAC can only be successful in tackling 'petty' [bureaucratic] corruption – and that, if the Committee tried to investigate cases of 'grand' corruption, party discipline would be invoked to ensure that the majority [governing] party MPs on the Committee would squash enquiries."

The challenge for committees is that they do not have prosecutorial powers. A variety of follow-up mechanisms were described by respondents. Some said that the committees make recommendations to the House which often calls for the parties involved to make amends and/or be prosecuted. Others said that the committee's findings are transmitted to the Attorney General's department for prosecution, referred to the police for investigation, or the Serious Frauds Office (SFO), or the Commission for Human Rights and Administrative Justice (CHRAJ); in the case of the latter two organisations, see above. In short, the committees in Parliament have to rely on multiple agencies and channels for further action, including prosecution of their findings.

A problem with follow-up is that ultimately it is the office of the Attorney General (AG) that is responsible for prosecution. The AG's mandate is governed by Article 88 of the 1992 constitution, under which the AG doubles as a Minister of State and principal legal counselor to the government. As Minister of State, the AG is part of the executive branch – and, at the same time, is responsible for prosecutions emanating from the investigations of parliament and its committees, the Serious Frauds Office (SFO) and the Auditor General. In short, some respondents said, the contribution of the AG to parliamentary oversight is dampened by the perception that the office is not independent; they were of the opinion that some cases were not prosecuted, possibly because of political interference and influence.

In short, the committees are able to perform their functions because they are constitutionally empowered to access information and subpoena witnesses. By holding open sessions and allowing public and media access, the committees have increased incentives for greater scrutiny. The composition and selection of committee members demonstrates a tendency towards independence and autonomy which is applauded by experts (see, for example, Wang, 2005). While committee resources are limited, ties have been developed with policy think tanks and input from the public encouraged. Finally, although partisanship is strong in Parliament, the collective interest of MPs seems to supersede party affiliation at the committee level. The ability of MPs to minimise partisanship at the committee level has helped make the committees powerful vehicles in the oversight process.

Given the greater activism and the greater effectiveness of parliament and parliamentary committees in performing their oversight function, it is not terribly surprising to find out that parliament is regarded as a highly trusted institution. According to Afrobarometer surveys,[19] public confidence in the Parliament of Ghana appears to be strong. Electoral turnout is high (87 per cent in 2004) and 67 per cent knew the name of their Member of Parliament. One third of Ghanaians believe their country to be a "full democracy" while a further 49 per cent believe it to be a democracy with minor (38 per cent) or major (11 per cent) problems. Eighty-five per cent of Ghanaians would either strongly disapprove or disapprove of parliament being abolished so that the President could decide everything.

Sixty eight per cent of Ghanaians reported at least "some" or "a lot" of trust in parliament, behind the President (75 per cent) and the army (72 per cent) but above the Electoral Commission, the Local Assembly (55 per cent), independent newspapers (48 per cent) and the law courts (63 per cent).

Similarly, the public believed Members of Parliament to be less corrupt than local and national government officials, local government councilors, the police, tax officials and judges/magistrates but more corrupt than health workers, teachers or the President and officials in his office (see table 6.3).

Section three: what makes parliament work better?

Respondents provided several answers as to why the Parliament of Ghana has been so effective in performing oversight activities. One such reason is that partisanship at the committee level is weak, scoring a mean of 2.3 on a scale of 1–5, where 1 = very weak and 5 = very strong, thereby permitting a more collegial atmosphere for deliberation – although MPs considered there to be less partisanship than did parliamentary staff, civil society representatives and journalists. Various reasons were offered for the absence of partisanship

Table 6.3 How many of the following people do you think are involved in corruption?

	Most/all	Some
President and officials in his office	56	16
Members of parliament	59	16
Local government councilors	60	19
National government officials	67	26
Local government officials	67	27
Police	80	51
Tax officials	71	35
Judges and magistrates	72	35
Health workers	58	17
Teachers and school administrators	57	17

Source: Afrobarometer 2005 survey reported in briefing paper no. 20, November 2005, available online at www.afrobarometer.org.

at the committee level. Some interviewees thought that at the committee level, national interest is supreme and MPs are more oriented towards achieving broad national goals than parochial party interests. But also suggested were issues of collegiality, resulting from working together in small groups on issues.

The relative absence of partisanship at the committee level is worthy of further investigation. Respondents indicated that, in a few cases partisanship overshadowed the work of committees. This suggests that there may be "triggers" of partisanship at the committee level. Although we did not probe our respondents for what these triggers might be, our document search suggests that partisanship may coincide with issues before the House permitting the minority to use visible national issues to distinguish itself from the majority ruling party. For example, the government's planned sale in 2008 of 70 per cent ownership of the national telecommunications company, Ghana Telecom, to Vodafone International BV of the Netherlands generated tense disagreements between the majority and minority parties in parliament. The government argued that the sale was intended to inject private ownership into the ailing telecommunications company and improve its management. But the minority party and other civil society groups rejected the government's claim because the $900 million amount representing the 70 per cent ownership of Ghana Telecom grossly undervalued the company. The selling price raised suspicions and led to accusations about the government's sincerity and openness in the privatisation deal. In addition, questions were raised about the government's publicly stated objective for the sale. The minority party quoted a celebrated economist and member of the ruling New Patriotic Party, Kwame Pianim, who had been quoted in a *Daily Graphic* newspaper report that the government urgently needed an infusion of cash to strengthen the macro economy and control inflation. This issue divided the legislature along party lines. Parliament failed to pass the bill authorising the sale before it went on recess in July 2008. In August 2008 parliament was recalled from recess to approve the sale. The bill authorising the sale passed after four hours of debate by a majority vote of 124 yeas and 74 nays.

The conclusion that the effectiveness of committees and committee work is inversely related to the level of partisanship or, to put it in a different way, that partisanship is detrimental to the success of oversight activities, was indirectly confirmed by another set of findings on what makes special/*ad hoc* committees work well.[20] Even in this respect, our respondents provided a mixed evaluation of the performance of special committees. Their general impression is that the effectiveness of committees depends on their composition: they are effective when evenly composed of members of both parties but ineffective when packed with members of the majority party.

A second factor that facilitates the success of legislative oversight in the Parliament of Ghana is, paradoxically, the lack of adequate resources and research staff in the parliament. To compensate for this lack of "in house" resources, many parliamentary committees and individual MPs have ties to policy think tanks; those mentioned include the Ghana Centre for Democratic Development (CDD), the Institute of Economic Affairs (IEA), the Institute for Democratic Governance (IDEG), Legal Resources Centre (LRC), Integrated Social Development Centre (ISODEC), Canada Investment Fund for Africa (CIFA), Country Environmental Analysis (CEA), the Faculty of Law – University of Ghana, and the Parliamentary Centre of Canada – The African Poverty Reduction Network.[21] These think tanks contribute to enhancing the knowledge of MPs and parliamentary staff through workshops and seminars on proposed policies and issues which come before committees.

This nexus between MPs, parliamentary staff and think tanks often leads to an 'opening up' of the policy process to the public and greater interaction between MPs and civil society groups. Often, the policy think tanks will organise parliamentary-civil society forums to facilitate public interaction on proposed policy changes, for example, the asset declaration law, education on conflict of interest law, and African Union/United Nations convention on corruption were supported by ISODEC, CEA, Faculty of Law-University of Ghana respectively. Recently, ISODEC assisted MPs by preparing background papers, policy analysis, soliciting civic input and explaining technical points, such as the work on the Millennium Challenge Account bill. MPs are also assisted by these groups to improve their oversight duties through field visits.

A note of caution must be sounded. Many of these think tanks are committed to particular issue areas ranging from economics, law, poverty alleviation, social development, water, environment and so on, and it is possible that MPs are only receiving input from well-organised advocacy groups. By organising seminars for MPs these organisations are able not only to inform MPs but also to lobby them to support legislation in particular issue areas.

The third condition that facilitated the successful performance of legislative oversight is represented by what Pelizzo and Stapenhurst (2007) called, for lack of a better term, demand for good governance. Lindberg and Zhou (2009) argued that after relatively strong and increasing oversight during the period 1992 through about 2000, the Ghanaian Parliament's oversight – and other functions vis-à-vis the executive[22] – function weakened, as a result of both structural factors and persons involved.[23] Our assessment suggests a reversal in this apparent decline. The PAC became active, more public and is believed to be increasingly more effective.[24]

Similarly, the vetting process of ministerial appointments, also widely reported in both the press and by broadcast media, is bringing the issue of parliamentary oversight to the fore while Question Period appears to be becoming more substantive and is attracting media coverage. One respondent claimed that " … increased media coverage of parliament – and especially PAC public hearings – is resulting in citizens demanding more from their MPs which is causing MPs to sit up and deliver" and this, in turn, creates the conditions for more effective oversight.

Conclusion

By focusing on what makes legislative oversight effective in Ghana, we have addressed some of the issues that were not adequately addressed by the first wave of studies in comparative constitutional engineering. In fact, in contrast to what the first generation of comparative constitutional engineers has generally argued, namely that only macro-institutions (that is, form of government) matter, we are able to show that meso-institutions matter as well. The success of Ghana in overseeing the executive, curbing/preventing corruption, improving governance and in increasing the legitimacy of the Fourth Republic are not only determined by the form of government established by the Constitution but also by the fact that the legislature both has a variety of oversight tools at its disposal and puts these to good use. Hence, we believe that the first lesson to be learned from this chapter is that meso-level institutions are more important than previous comparative constitutional engineers had acknowledged. But at the same time, the importance of meso-level institutions should not be exaggerated. As we noted in Chapters 3, 4 and 5, the range of oversight tools at the disposal of a legislature only determines that legislature's oversight potential, but is by itself insufficient to ensure that such oversight potential is translated into actual oversight or, even better, into effective oversight.

The second lesson that can be drawn from this chapter is that in the Ghanaian case it is possible to detect a positive relationship between an increase in the amount of oversight activities performed by the legislature and the reputation of parliament and parliamentarians, the legitimacy of democracy and political institutions, and the success in curbing/preventing corruption. In fact, we were able to show that as the amount of oversight activities performed by the legislature increased (or at least was perceived to be increasing by the respondents and the public), so did the reputation and the legitimacy of parliament. We noted, however, that while parliament became more active in certain areas (for example, confirmation of appointments), in other areas (censure on ministers) parliament's activity has either not increased or the increase of activity performed (number of parliamentary questions asked) came at the expense of quality of the activity – which raises serious questions as to the parliament's ability to perform effectively certain tasks.

This leads to the third lesson, namely that institutions, regardless of whether they are macro- or meso-, do not operate in a vacuum and that their successful functioning depends, as Rockman (1984) observed long ago, on the presence/absence of specific contextual conditions.[25] With regard to the success of legislative oversight in Ghana, we identified three such conditions: a relatively low level of partisanship, parliament's ability to find alternative sources of information, and the demand for good governance.

Building on the conclusions from this and previous chapters, we are ready to develop our comprehensive model of legislative oversight, which we present in Chapter 7.

7 A strategic interaction model

Introduction

The literature on oversight has been generally oblivious to the theory of agency and the importance of voter demands. As we have noted in Chapter 3, legislative oversight scholars have produced a wide range of explanations for why oversight may be effective. Some scholars have underlined the importance of the legal framework, the (range of) formal powers assigned to the overseeing bodies, the size of the staff at the disposal of the overseeing authorities, the salience of the issues and so on. In other words, they have either reduced oversight effectiveness to the status of a random event (when the issue is salient, oversight is effective, otherwise it is not) or they have viewed it as a quasi-deterministic consequence of a set of structural conditions.

Yet, neither position is particularly appealing. The fatalistic explanation (oversight is effective when it is effective) is disappointing on theoretical grounds as it fails even to qualify as a pseudo-scientific form of theorising. The deterministic explanation is also disappointing on theoretical grounds because, while it is inappropriate to suggest that oversight effectiveness and capacity are orthogonal, it is equally incorrect to suggest that they are linked in a deterministic way.

Therefore, structural conditions alone are insufficient to explain why oversight capacity is sometimes used effectively by legislatures. Structural conditions may facilitate effective oversight, but they cannot cause it.

In this chapter we formulate an agential explanation of oversight effectiveness. Our explanation is fairly straightforward: the adoption of oversight mechanisms must be viewed as a subsample of a broader social scientific phenomenon, namely institutional change. The effective use of oversight tools must be viewed as a subsample of why newly established institutions are successful in generating the results for which they had been established. In other words, in order to understand both the adoption and the effective use of oversight tools, we propose a theory of institutional change and performance. Specifically, we suggest that voter demands play a key role in shaping the set of incentives confronting political actors as well as their strategies and choices. We claim that it is the interplay between voter demands and politicians' strategic considerations that explains why oversight capacity is or is not used effectively.

This chapter is organised in the following way. In the first section we discuss theories of institutional change, building on our initial review in Chapter 2. In doing so, we note that institutional change has been explained on the grounds of micro, macro and micro-macro approaches, that all these approaches agree that institutional change generally occurs as a response to a crisis (real or perceived) and that crises are viewed either as exogenous or endogenous shocks. Building on this discussion we go on to argue that for "New Development Economics" the successful performance of newly established institutions depends on whether or not the newly adopted institutions are a domestic response to an endogenous crisis. When the newly established institutions are a domestic response to such a crisis, the newly established institutions perform successfully. By contrast, when the newly established institutions are a foreign solution that is borrowed or copied to cope with the crisis, the performance of newly established institutions is far from successful.

In the second section, we propose an alternative model of institutional change and performance. In doing so, we argue that efforts to alter institutional arrangements are usually made in response to a crisis (real or perceived), that such a crisis creates a strategic situation in which the ruling elite and reformers interact and in which a substantive institutional change is only one of several possible outcomes. Crises allow the ruling elite to neglect the reformist demands altogether, they may force the ruling elite to make only cosmetic changes to the institutional system or they may force the ruling elite to make substantive institutional reforms. We will argue that substantive reforms occur only when neglecting the reformist demands of the population would bring the ruling elite into disrepute, erode its – and the political system's – legitimacy, and possibly create the conditions for a system-wide breakdown.

In the third and final section, we will draw some tentative conclusions.

Section one: understanding institutional change: the story so far

The literature on institutional change is divided into three streams: the macro-level, the micro-level and the bi (micro-macro)-level.

Macro-level explanations provide several different, and sometimes conflicting, explanations for why institutional change occurs: structural conditions, culture, institutions, ideas and individual preferences are all invoked as determinants of change. Yet, none of these factors manages to provide *per se* a fully convincing explanation. There are several reasons for this. In particular, they risk "explanatory determinism, ignoring possibly independent influences of actors and their strategic interactions on political outcomes" (Knill and Lenschow, 2001: 194). That is, they all see change, to recall Blyth's (2002) criticism of structural explanations of institutional change "as a problem of comparative statics". Structural explanations, Blyth suggested, "implicitly posit the model: 'institutional equilibrium- > punctuation- > new institutional equilibrium" (Blyth, 2002: 7). This means that structural arguments explain the two equilibria as if they were simply the necessary outcome of a new set of structural conditions. Such an argument is somewhat problematic.

In this respect, Blyth (2002:7) noted that "unless one can specify the causal links between the former and the latter objects", the *post hoc*, *propter hoc* logic does not explain much. This is true, but is not the only problem. A structural explanation of political change may be plagued by other potential problems: it may be circular (a change explains a change), it may be spurious (both changes are in reality the product of some other and unobserved forces) and it may be a *regressio ad infinitum*. A change can always be explained by a previous change.

A very similar criticism could also be made, by extension, also for the other macro-level explanations, such as the cultural and ideational modes of explanation. Cultural arguments tend to explain social, economic and political phenomena on the basis of cultural values that are assumed to be fairly stable over time. This creates a problem as to the cultural approach's ability to address change.[1] In fact, by assuming that cultural values are constant over time and by assuming that they are the "real" determinants of social and political phenomena, social and political changes can then be explained only on the basis of cultural changes. This, of course, brings us back to the same problems encountered with regard to the structural explanation. Cultural explanations of change run the serious risk of being circular, or regressing ad infinitum, or being spurious.

Ideational explanations suggest that institutional change is just the outcome of an ideational struggle. According to Blyth (2002), the triumph in the ideational struggle is what determines a shift in the ideational paradigm, that is, in the dominant way of viewing things. In this respect, the shift in the ideational paradigm resembles the shift in the scientific paradigm that characterises scientific revolutions. However, between the ideational struggle theorised by Blyth (2002) and the clash of scientific paradigms, there are some major differences. The triumph of a new scientific paradigm is ultimately due to the fact that the new scientific paradigm explains more and better than its competitors, whereas in Blyth's (2002) understanding of the triumph of a new paradigm over its competitors is the result of a mobilisation of resources, not of the fact that it works better than its competitors. Thus, the real determinant of institutional change is not so much the quality of ideas but the mobilisation of resources employed to disseminate certain ideas. In other words, the success of ideational forces is viewed as a quasi-mechanistic, quasi-deterministic product of material forces. This point has two basic implications: first the ideational explanation is spurious and all but ideational; second, if the institutional change is a consequence of a change in the ideational paradigm and if the change in the institutional paradigm is a consequence of a change in the distribution of material resources, the ideational explanation ends up explaining a change with a change – just like the theories it wanted to criticise. And, finally, ideational explanations tend to pay insufficient attention to the real drivers of institutional change: political actors or agents.

The alternative to these macro-level arguments is represented by micro-level explanations of change that adopt agency as the single most important determinant of change, initially considered in Chapter 2. Institutional change is produced by what Mahoney and Snyder (1999: 5) call the "ongoing interactions between purposeful actors" whose ability to achieve their goals is potentially limited by structures and structural incentives. Mahoney and Snyder (1999) went on to argue that while both micro- and macro-level theories of institutional change view it as the product of the interaction between structural and agential factors, structuralists tend to oversocialise agents, while (micro-) voluntarist theories tend to undersocialise agents.

This is why, in spite of the fact that the micro approach acknowledges that agents and political actors are not atoms floating in the vacuum, their options, choices and behaviour may be constrained by structural conditions, it has been criticised for the belief

> that elite bargaining over new arrangements occurs on a tabula rasa, without regard to entrenched understandings and power relationships ... actors change goals and perceptions in response to uncertainty and bargain in a dynamic way – producing different outcomes ... But elites work from power positions and understandings embedded in inherited arrangements; indeed, they try to encode those older meanings and power relationships into seemingly new structures.
>
> (Skocpol, 2003: 423)

In other words, Skocpol criticised micro-explanations for failing to grasp that institutional change may be formal or cosmetic but not substantive and suggested that more attention should be paid to the embeddedness of institutions (Granovetter, 1985).

In spite of this methodological pluralism, the literature agreed unanimously on one point: demands for institutional reforms arise when the previous institutional order suffers a crisis or a breakdown, which, in its turn, may be exogenous or endogenous. Electoral reforms, the transformation of party finance legislation, constitutional reforms are all generally enacted as a response to a crisis: the electoral system's inability to provide adequate representation of voter preferences; political parties' loss of legitimacy; and the government instability/ineffectiveness.

Scholars have disagreed, however, as to what makes institutional reforms work successfully. For the ideationalists an institutional change is successful because it occurs, it occurs because it was able to create a better narrative than its competitors, and because it could mobilise more resources for disseminating such narratives, thus making it hegemonic. But the ideationalists are not terribly interested in whether the institutional reform is successful in the sense of solving the problems the crisis had generated. For those who believe that an institutional change represents a response to an exogenous shock, whether the institutional change is a domestic or a foreign response to the crisis has little to no effect as to whether the institutional change will solve the problems the crisis had generated. For them an institutional change is successful when it is able to solve the problems that had emerged in the crisis. For the "New Development Economists", institutional change can occur for a variety of reasons, in response to either exogenous or endogenous shocks, and it can be either a domestic or a foreign solution, but they go on to say institutional change is successful in getting the problems solved only when the institutional change is a domestic solution for an endogenous shock.[2] In other words, an institution is successful, to paraphrase Boettke and Storr (2002: 163) only when it evolves naturally from a socially embedded foundation.[3]

Section two: our explanation

In our model there are two sets of actors: the members of the ruling elite and the members of society. Whether an institutional reform occurs or not, and whether a newly established institution succeeds in eliminating the problems that emerged in the course of the crisis or not, depends on the interaction of these two groups.

A corruption scandal, an economic crisis, the alleged mismanagement of public resources, the unethical behaviour of the ruling elite may all erode the legitimacy of the ruling elite and of the political system. In response to this crisis, citizens and social groups may voice their discontent with the functioning of the political system and they may demand political reforms and institutional changes to eliminate the problems that the crisis disclosed.

The ruling elite, confronted with these popular demands, faces two options: it may decide to preserve the status quo or it may decide to make some institutional reforms. The ruling elite's decision to reform or not to reform the political system depends on how strong the ruling elite is (or, at least, on how strong it believes itself to be), on how strong the ruling elite believes society and social demands to be. If the ruling elite believes that it is strong enough to neglect social demands without having to pay the price for such a choice, the ruling elite will decide to preserve the status quo. Whereas, if the ruling elite believes that an effort to preserve the status quo may exacerbate the crisis, further delegitimising the ruling class, and potentially leading to more disastrous changes such as civil conflict or military coup, the ruling elite will agree to make some institutional changes.

Furthermore, at this stage, the ruling elite may still be very much convinced that any institutional reform will be purely formal and cosmetic, that it will not amount to any meaningful change and that it will not produce a substantive change in how the political system operates.

Once the ruling elite enacts the institutional reforms, society is left with two basic choices: to regard the reforms as a political success, to be satisfied by what it was able to achieve and drop additional demands or alternatively to articulate further demands. If society makes the first choice, the reforms are enacted but they are fairly ineffective in tackling the problems for which they had been demanded in the first place. If society makes the second choice, it puts the ruling elite in a very difficult position. In fact, if society demands additional, or more incisive, reforms, the ruling elite is left with three unappealing prospects: to ensure that the newly established reforms perform effectively, in which case the reforms succeed and the ruling elite may lose some of the benefits it had previously enjoyed in the status quo ante; to neglect the new social demands and run the risk of losing whatever legitimacy it has left, thereby creating the conditions for a further crisis; or, finally, to ignore popular demands, tolerate unethical and corrupt behaviour and the suboptimal functioning of the newly established institutions at the risk, once again, of compromising its legitimacy as well as that of the political system as a whole. The model is presented in figure 7.1.

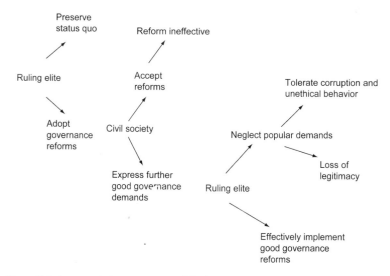

Figure 7.1 A strategic interaction model of institutional change and performance

As should be clear, our position differs from previous explanations. Unlike the macro-level explanations of change, we do not believe that institutional change can be accounted for simply in terms of structural, cultural, social or ideational factors. Similarly, micro-level explanations tend to overestimate the importance of voluntaristic factors and to underestimate social constraints, power relations and legacies from the status quo ante. Thus, our model emphasises that actors change preferences, choices and strategies in response to changing circumstances, that they interact in a dynamic way and that such interactions do not occur in a vacuum but are instead influenced, not deterministically, by previous understandings and power relations. Furthermore, our model differs from a Washington consensus that treats institutional change and performance as a consequence of exogenous shocks and it also differs from the New Development Economics approach for we do not believe that the success of an institutional reform is a necessary consequence of domestic/endogenous nature.

Our model makes it quite clear that the success of institutional reforms is independent of whether they are domestic or foreign solutions. In fact, our model illustrates why domestic solutions that are adopted to respond to a domestic/endogenous crisis may fail just as foreign solutions that are enacted in response to an exogenous shock. Indeed, our model shows that if the political elite is not given a strong incentive to reform the political system, it will resist efforts to change the status quo. Therefore, the question does not concern so much whether the crisis is exogenous or endogenous or whether the institutional response to a crisis is foreign or domestic. The real question is whether an institutional reform is carried out as a mere formality or whether it is carried out to substantively alter the way in which the political system operates. Whether institutional reforms are formal or substantive depends on the strategic interplay between political elites and the rest of society – because it is only through this interplay that the ruling elite may be induced to accept both formal and substantive institutional change.

Section three: conclusions

In Chapters 5 and 6 we tested some beliefs that had guided the international organisation and practitioners devoted to either democracy or development promotion, namely that oversight effectiveness was essential for promoting democracy and reducing corruption, that oversight effectiveness could be enhanced by expanding oversight capacity. While the results of our statistical analyses revealed that while effective oversight was a major determinant of the quality of democracy and of the level of corruption, they did not sustain the claim that oversight effectiveness is simply a function of oversight capacity and, as a consequence, did not sustain the claim that by expanding the oversight capacity at the disposal of legislature, the effectiveness of oversight activities will be boosted. In the course of those two chapters it was noted oversight is effective when oversight tools are used effectively.

While in those two chapters we did not address why oversight capacity sometimes leads to effective oversight activity and in some other cases it does not, this chapter was entirely focused on the determinants of oversight effectiveness or effective oversight activity. We have proposed a strategic interaction model which explains what makes legislative oversight effective and what ensures that oversight tools are put to effective use. These issues reflect a more general problem of institutional change, which in our view can be broken down into two distinct issues: Why does institutional change/reform occur in some cases but not in others and why do newly established institutions function in some cases but not in others? Building on the very large and important body of scholarly work, we have suggested that both institutional reforms and institutional performance can be explained on the basis of a strategic interaction model.

In its basic features, the model posits that in the wake of a legitimacy crisis there is a popular demand to address the critical elements, and institutional reform occurs when the ruling elite decides to address and satisfy, at least formally, the popular demands. We noted that while this part of the model explains why institutional change occurs, it provides no evidence as to how institutions will perform. In this second respect we noted that once institutional change has occurred, the newly established institution will perform well or not depending on whether civil society is satisfied by the institutional reform at the formal level or whether it seeks substantive change. In this latter case, our model posits, a newly established institution performs effectively.

We argued that this model can be applied to institutional change and reforms in general but also to the expansion of oversight capacity, that is, to the adoption of additional oversight tools. We further argued that this model provides a compelling explanation for why oversight tools/capacity are sometimes used effectively and sometimes not. We believe that the proposed theory is of some interest to scholars and practitioners alike. It is important for scholars devoted to the study of institutions and institutional change, because our model provides an explanation that is parsimonious, logically consistent, easily testable, easily falsifiable, without, however, being too formalistic to be applied to the analysis of concrete empirical cases. It is important for comparative legislative studies specialists because it is one of the first attempts to explain oversight effectiveness on the basis of a micro-level explanation.

In the next chapter, we test our theory using empirical data that has been collected in two surveys of PACs undertaken by the World Bank Institute (WBI). We use these data to show that explanations developed previously do not provide convincing explanations for why PACs work effectively. These explanations argued that PAC performance reflects the size, the formal powers, the partisan composition, the institutionalisation, the partisan affiliation of the chairperson. By contrast, application of our theory reveals that none of these factors matters much. If these factors are fixed, they cannot account for within-country variation over time – at best they can be used to explain cross-country variation. Yet, the problem we are confronted with is: Why do we detect variations of a particular PAC's performance over time? This can only be explained by abandoning a static, macro-level focus in favour of a micro-approach such as ours.

8   Testing the model – Public Accounts Committees

Introduction

In this chapter we test the theoretical model presented in Chapter 7. We do so by focusing on the adoption and the performance of a specific oversight tool: the Public Account Committee (PAC). This chapter comprises four sections.

In section one we provide an in-depth discussion of what PACs are, what they do and why they are believed to be a cornerstone of any effort to promote government accountability. Given the relatively large and growing body of research on this topic, we provide, in section two, a fairly exhaustive discussion of what are believed to be the most important determinants of PACs' activity and successful performance. Building on this review, in section three we go on to show that most of the structural, institutional, macro-level explanations of PACs' activity do not explain much either in statistical or in theoretical terms, as they fail to provide a compelling reason for why political actors decide to use/not to use effectively the powers assigned to a PAC and to make the committee perform effectively. In section four we demonstrate that the strategic interaction model presented in the previous chapter is superior to the theoretical approaches adopted heretofore in explaining these issues. It provides an explanation of why the political will to make PACs perform effectively emerges from a strategic interaction between various political actors in a given polity.

Section one: diffusion of Public Accounts Committees

The international community and international organisations such as the World Bank, the United Nations Development Program (UNDP) and International Development Law Organization (IDLO), to name just a few, have identified the absence of government accountability as a main obstacle to successful socio-economic development, the improvement of democratic quality and the consolidation of democracy. Among the vehicles for better accountability, the strengthening of parliaments and legislatures is seen as a key component to promote good governance and keep governments accountable. These beliefs are based on a simple proposition: *if parliaments and legislatures can oversee government activity, then governance will be improved* (Stapenhurst and Pelizzo, 2002).

Within that proposition is nested a second assumption. Since financial oversight has long been the traditional cornerstone of accountability, effective oversight of expenditure is an essential *sine qua non* of good governance - by which we mean the capacity of parliaments to scrutinise government finances. Traditionally, in the former British colonies and in the countries of the (British) Commonwealth, there is a specific parliamentary committee, called Public Account Committee (PAC), that performs the task of overseeing and scrutinising government expenditures. The purpose of such a committee is not so much to question government policy but rather to ensure that policies enacted by the executive are implemented in an economic, efficient and effective manner.

Given this, international organisations, practitioners and legislative studies scholars have paid increasing attention to PACs. A growing body of research has addressed a variety of issues, topics and questions. Some studies have investigated the legislative or normative dispositions under which PACs are established and operate (KPMG, 2006), the size of PACs (McInnes, 1977; McGee, 2002), the selection of PACs' Chairpersons (McGee, 2002), or the powers and the functions of the committee (KPMG, 2006); they have all done so in order to identify what makes PACs work effectively (Pelizzo *et al.*, 2006). These studies were carried out as synchronic one-country case studies, as diachronic one-country case-studies (Degeling, Anderson and Guthrie, 1996; Jacobs, Jones and Smith, 2010), as small-sample comparative analyses, as within-region comparative analyses (Pelizzo, 2010a) or as large-sample comparative analyses (McGee, 2002; Pelizzo *et al.*, 2006). In spite of their many differences, all these studies had one aspect in common: they all focused on PACs operating in countries that had been British colonies and were part of the (British) Commonwealth. Of course, some scholars had been quick to note that, from an organisational point of view, the PAC followed either the British or the Australian model. In the former, the Chair of the PAC is assigned to an MP from the Opposition, while in the latter it is assigned to an MP from the Government. But the existence of such organisational difference did not alter the fact that, regardless of whether PACs were modelled after the Australian or the British archetype, PACs could only be found in countries that had been British colonies and which followed, broadly speaking, the "Westminster" system of parliamentary governance.

Recent years have, however, witnessed the diffusion of PACs (or their functional equivalents) to countries beyond the (British) Commonwealth (Samsudin and Mohamed, 2009). They can now be found in Afghanistan, Bhutan, Denmark, Ethiopia, the Federated States of Micronesia, Finland, Indonesia, Kosovo, Liberia, Nepal, Rwanda and Thailand.

Preliminary efforts to explain the diffusion of PACs outside the British Commonwealth have tested whether the diffusion of the PAC could be explained on the basis of three theoretical frameworks – an historical one, a rational choice one and a sociological one. In their analysis, Hamilton and Stapenhurst (2011) found that historical legacies matter little in determining whether a country adopts a PAC or not. Furthermore, they found that structurally and organisationally, the PACs established outside the (British) Commonwealth resemble fairly closely the PACs that operate in the countries within the Commonwealth. While this evidence is fairly interesting, since it shows that similar if not identical structures can be transplanted (and survive) in different institutional contexts, it does not sustain the claim advanced by Hamilton and Stapenhurst (2011) that PACs work equally well inside and outside the Commonwealth. While the authors may be correct in formulating this claim, the evidence provides little support. As one of us has argued elsewhere (Pelizzo, 2010b), and as we argue below, the relationship between the organisational and structural characteristics of PACs does not have a deterministic impact on the amount of activities performed by these committees or on whether such activities are carried out efficiently and effectively. Finally, Hamilton and Stapenhurst (2011) claim that the evidence at their disposal does not allow them to adjudicate whether the adoption of a PAC beyond the Commonwealth is best explained by rational choice or by sociological institutionalism, by the fact that the ruling elite enacts some institutional reforms out of sheer self-interest or under the pressure of social groups at the elite and at the mass level.

The strategic interaction model we presented in Chapter 7 is better than any of the approaches that were tested by Hamilton and Stapenhurst (2011). Our model explains more and explains better: it does not assume that actors (ruling elite or civil society groups) act in a vacuum, nor does it assume that the preferences/choices/strategies of these actors are fixed over time. Rather, it makes it clear that political actors interact in a dynamic way, by constantly modifying their behaviour and strategy in response to what is done by their counterparts. Furthermore, it explains something that neither the rational choice theorists nor the sociological-institutionalism theorists are able to explain, namely why ruling elites, that for a long time had little interest in reforming the institutional system, for instance by adopting a PAC, at some point decided to do so.

Of course, one could say that the decision to adopt a PAC could be stimulated by an exogenous stimulus. The international community may feel that corruption represents a major obstacle for a country's socio-economic development, creates pressure on that country's political class to take some active steps to curb corruption and recommends, among other measures, the adoption of a PAC, and the country in question changes the parliamentary committee system by adopting a PAC or a functionally equivalent committee. While perfectly plausible and logical, this explanation is somewhat problematic. In fact, if the adoption of a PAC were simply a response to an exogenous stimulus of this kind, PACs should be more widespread than they are and they should be found in all the countries in which international organisations promote anti-corruption programmes and activities. Yet, this is far from being the case. Many countries that have high levels of corruption have not felt the need to take significant steps to fight corruption or to adopt a PAC.

Our model can explain why this is the case. A country's political elite is willing to launch a set of institutional reforms only when its survival as ruling class is at risk. It is only when a crisis occurs and the political system is losing legitimacy and needs to take some active steps to regain citizen trust that the reforms are enacted. To paraphrase what we wrote earlier (Pelizzo and Stapenhurst, 2006: 198), the adoption of reforms (such as the establishment of a PAC) represents an attempt to rebuild the public trust in the political system. In the absence of such a crisis, reformist pressures from the international community and from civil society will not persuade the ruling class, who have a vested interest in the preservation of the status quo, to make any institutional changes.

The claim that reforms (such as the adoption of a PAC) are a response to crises of legitimacy is supported by empirical evidence. Indonesia has recently established a PAC to scrutinise government expenditure, reduce corruption, preserve/improve citizen trust of parliament and prevent the de-legitimisation of parliament and of the other democratic institutions. Similarly, in Thailand where democracy collapsed in 2006 in the midst of a corruption crisis, a PAC has been established to improve the level of governance and create firmer conditions for the consolidation and the survival of the newly established democracy. Much in the same vein, a PAC was created in Ethiopia in 2006 as part of a government attempt to diffuse political tensions that engulfed the country following the 2005 national elections. Specifically, it was established in order to bolster the role of parliament following allegations over election irregularities and an attempt, by the outgoing parliament, to weaken the ability of opposition parties to fully participate in parliamentary procedures.

In other words, legitimacy crisis may occur for a wide variety of reasons.[1] They may be due to a corruption scandal, to a patent abuse of power, to what the population regards as unacceptable violations of the democratic rules. Whenever a legitimacy crisis occurs, the ruling elite no longer has the power to preserve the status quo, it is under popular pressure to signal its awareness of popular demands, and therefore it accepts, however reluctantly, the reformist process.

This stylised account provides an explanation for why or rather under what circumstances institutional reforms occur. This account could explain a variety of institutional reforms, ranging from party finance legislation (or the abolition thereof), electoral reforms, constitutional reforms, as well as the anti-corruption reforms such as the adoption of a PAC.[2]

Section two: determining factors of PAC success – the story so far

While the literature and, more importantly, the international community have long regarded the PAC as a necessary tool in the fight against misallocation of resources and corruption, they have also long acknowledged that there is great variation in the effectiveness of PAC performance and a growing body of research has addressed the question, "What makes PACs work effectively?"

Scholars and practitioners have formulated several answers to this question. They have suggested that the successful performance is the result of how the PAC is institutionalised, of the legislative/normative framework under which it operates, of its organisational features (size, Chairmanship), of its partisan composition, of the range of its formal powers, of the focus of its investigations and of the context in which it operates. We review each answer/explanation in turn. In doing so we will not simply list which factors have been regarded as significant determinants of PAC performance but we will also provide empirical, or rather statistical, evidence to show whether and to what extent such factors are actually responsible for oversight effectiveness.

PAC performance and legislative dispositions

Some studies have underlined that the performance of a PAC is affected by the legislative/normative framework under which it operates. Scholars who have emphasised the importance of legislative dispositions can be divided into two groups: those who believe that normative dispositions matter unconditionally and those who believe instead that the normative dispositions matter only under certain conditions.

Those scholars who believe in the unconditional importance of the normative framework under which a PAC operates in shaping its performance can be further divided into two sub-groups: one group comprises those who believe that PACs operate more effectively when they are established by constitutional dispositions and less effectively otherwise (Rawlings, 2006: 5), while the second group believes that PACs operate more effectively when they are established by an act of parliament (Jacobs, Jones and Smith, 2010).

In contrast to those scholars who believe that the performance of PACs is a direct consequence of the legislative framework under which they operate, other scholars yet again have stressed that the relationship between norms and rules on the one hand and performance on the other hand is conditional. One of the best examples of this group is provided by Hardman (1984a, 1984b, 1986) who argued that legislative and normative dispositions boost the performance of a PAC on the condition that such norms and dispositions are domestic responses to endogenous needs.

Echoing what in the late 1970s were the Hayekian notions of spontaneous and self-generating order and what in the new millennium Boettke and Storr (2002) regard as domestic solutions for domestic problems, Hardman (1986) argued that "sedulous adherence to conventional Westminster forms and mechanisms in financial legislation on and after self-government ... precluded the emergence of innovatory measures specifically addressing indigenous development and cultural preservation". Hardman (1986) went on to argue that the financial legislation modelled after that of the former colonial powers was inadequate, that financial control was inefficient, and that more effective financial scrutiny could be provided by developing local solutions to local conditions. In other words, the adoption/establishment of PACs could not possibly be successful because of their reliance on neo-colonial models and suggested that "the present control model would benefit from a realist assessment of indigenous factors in accounting for foreign aid, provincial government and expenditure programs" (Hardman, 1984a: 90).

PAC performance and contextual conditions

By stating that the successful performance is favoured by the presence of appropriate contextual conditions, Hardman (1984a, 1984b, 1986)[3] anticipated a theme that was revived in the mid-1990s by Degeling, Anderson and Guthrie (1996), namely that the successful performance of a PAC depends on contextual factors.

Specifically, Degeling, Anderson and Guthrie (1996) identified six different foci of PAC investigations, noting that some have more bite than others. They also noted that PACs performing one type of scrutiny rather than another is a function of the existing legal dispositions, which in turn reflects different contextual conditions.[4] In their analysis of the Australian PACs over the period 1917–32, Degeling, Anderson and Guthrie (1996) went on to show how changes in contextual conditions affected both the quantity (outputs) and the quality of PAC activities (outcomes).

The importance of contextual conditions in securing/preventing the effective functioning of PACs was also discussed in several more recent studies. For instance, Pelizzo *et al.* (2006) concluded that the success of these committees depended not only on the formal powers at their disposal but also on the presence of what they defined as "conditional factors". Pelizzo and Stapenhurst (2007) identified two additional conditions for successful PAC performance: access to free and reliable information and the availability of qualified staff to support PAC work. This said, Pelizzo and Stapenhurst (2007) also showed that the importance of conditions factors varies across regions – what makes a PAC work well in one region is not what makes it work effectively in a different region.[5]

And finally, scholars have identified two behavioural factors that may hinder the effective performance of PACs: political actors and members of the ruling elite may not have the political will to make PACs work effectively (Rawlings, 2006) and there may be little to no demand for better government accountability. Pelizzo and Stapenhurst (2007: 392), in fact, suggested that "If there is no demand for good governance … by civil society, the political class has no incentive to use oversight mechanisms to check and possibly improve the quality of governance."

PAC performance and the range of formal power

Some studies have underlined that the performance of PACs reflects not only how they are institutionalised, whether they are established by an act of parliament or by a constitutional disposition, the presence/absence of specific contextual factors (such as independent information), but also the formal power assigned to the PACs themselves.

For instance, having defined the effective performance of a PAC with the frequency with which it is able to achieve some results, Pelizzo *et al.* (2006) showed that there is some variation in the frequency with which different types of results are reached.[6] Furthermore, they suggested that the formal powers assigned to a PAC make a difference as to how frequently policy-relevant results are achieved or not. A similar point was made in more recent studies conducted with larger samples of data.

The World Bank Institute (WBI) conducted a survey in 2009, in which respondents were asked to indicate how many times their PAC met, how many hearings the PAC held, how many self-initiated inquiries the PAC had completed and how many reports the PAC had produced in the previous three years. Pelizzo (2010a) used this data to construct an index of formal powers (FPI). The presence of each of the powers used for the construction of the index was treated as a dichotomous variable, which took values 1 and 0 (zero) depending on whether a PAC in one of the countries included in this sample had or did not have that particular power. The index was then constructed by adding all the responses and by dividing by the number of responses. After constructing this index, Pelizzo (2010a) went on to correlate the index with two sets of data: the amount of activities performed by the PACs and index of legislative effectiveness in overseeing expenditure of public funds.[7] His conclusions were clear: that parliaments' ability to oversee effectively the expenditure of public funds was strongly and positively related to the formal powers of the PACs. While this finding was consistent with the notion that *effective* oversight was to a large extent a function of oversight *capacity*, it also suggested that some of the variance in legislative effectiveness in overseeing public expenditures was due to factors other than formal powers.

A second study to assess the relationship between PAC performance and PACs' formal powers was carried out in a study of PACs' activity in the Pacific Island states. In this study (Pelizzo, 2010b), the author revised the FPI. Having recognised that the PACs' powers pertain to four distinct areas – concerning respectively, the right of access, accounts and operations, the right of examining the Auditor General's (AG) reports and the involvement in the operation of the AG – Pelizzo first computed an index of formal power for each of these areas and then aggregated the scores to generate an overall FPI. By correlating this overall FPI with the indicators of PAC activity that were collected in the Pacific Island states (number of committee meetings, number of hearings, number of completed inquiries), Pelizzo (2010b) found that the range of formal powers at the disposal of a PAC is a poor predictor of how active and how effective they are.

Both of Pelizzo's studies (2010 a and 2010b) sustained the claim that while the presence of a wider range of formal power, if used, may lead to effective oversight, it does not say much as to whether there is the political will to use such powers and therefore does not say much about whether these powers are used.[8]

PAC performance and the organisational factors

Depending on the data employed, different studies have reached different and somewhat contradictory conclusions as to what is the impact of organisation, staffing, partisan composition of a PAC and its performance.

Studies that have employed elite survey data (McGee, 2002; Pelizzo *et al.*, 2006) have emphasised that structural or organisational factors, such as the partisan composition of the PAC membership, the partisan affiliation of the PAC Chair, the size of the PAC and size of the staff helping the committee in performing its tasks and duties, play a key role in determining how well a PAC performs. When, however, one analyses the relationship between the structural features and the committee performance, one finds that the relationship between the above-mentioned structural, partisan, organisational features on the one hand and the performance of PACs on the other hand is much less clear. We demonstrate this in the next section.

Section three: PAC performance determinants revisited

The data presented in table 8.1, collected in 2002 by the WBI in collaboration with the World Bank's South Asia Financial Management group, provide some information with regard to several organisational features of 24 PACs from the (British) Commonwealth.[9] These data concern the partisan affiliation of the PAC Chair, the size of the committee, the partisan composition of the committee (measured on the basis of the number of opposition MPs serving in this committee) and the number of the staff supporting the committee.

The data reveal that there is remarkable variation among these PACs. While the vast majority of them are chaired by an MP who belongs to the opposition, 16.6 per cent of them are chaired by an MP who belongs to the government party/coalition. PACs vary not only in size and in the number of members serving on the committee but also and more importantly in terms of the number of opposition MPs who serve in the committee and the number of staff serving the committee. PACs have on average 11.6 members, but their membership varies from a minimum of just 2 MPs in Anguilla to a maximum of 25 members in Ghana. PACs display great variation also with regard to the number of opposition MPs serving on the committee. This number in fact varies from a minimum of 0 (zero) opposition members in Singapore to a maximum of 12 in Ghana. But more important than the sheer number of opposition MPs is the fact that, with the exception of Anguilla (where the membership on the committee is evenly split between government and opposition) and Grenada (where all members of the PAC are selected from the opposition), the opposition MPs are greatly outnumbered by

Table 8.1 Size, number of staffers and partisan affiliation of PACs' chairpersons by country

Country	Committee chaired by a member of the opposition	Size of thecommittee	Number of opposition MPs serving on the PAC	Number of members of staff
Botswana	Yes	8	3	3
Gambia	Yes	10	2	–
Ghana	Yes	25	12	2
Kenya	Yes	11	5	2
Mozambique	No	15	7	3
Namibia	Yes	12	4	1
Nigeria	Yes	9	4	18
South Africa	Yes	16	6	5
Tanzania	Yes	15	2	3
Zambia	Yes	8	5	8
Anguilla	Yes	2	1	1
Barbados	Yes	13	6	2
Belize	Yes	7	3	2
Cayman	No	5	2	0
Jamaica	Yes	11	5	3
Guyana	Yes	10	4	0
Grenada	Yes	5	5	0
Canada	Yes	17	8	4
Ireland	Yes	12	6	4
New Zealand	No	12	6	3
India	Yes	22	8	20
Pakistan	Yes	12	4	15
Sri Lanka	Yes	15	7	3
Singapore	No	8	0	1

government/coalition MPs. The problem is particularly acute in the African PACs. The number of opposition MPs is half the number of government-affiliated MPs in Namibia, is one-quarter in Gambia and is one-sixth in Tanzania. And finally, there is great variation in the number of staff members working for the PAC. This number varies from a minimum of 0 (zero) in Guyana and Grenada to a maximum of 20 in India.

PACs also display significant differences in terms of output and activity. Respondents were asked to indicate how many meetings the PAC had held in the previous three years. These responses were converted into a four point scale and can be viewed in table 8.2.

Fifty per cent of the respondents said that their PAC had met more than 50 times, about a quarter of the respondents said that their PAC

Table 8.2 Number of meetings and reports by country (1999–2002)

Country	Number of meetings	Number of reports
Botswana	1	1
Gambia	–	–
Ghana	4	2
Kenya	4	1
Mozambique	4	3
Namibia	2	2
Nigeria	4	4
South Africa	4	4
Tanzania	2	1
Zambia	–	–
Anguilla	1	1
Barbados	1	1
Belize	1	1
Cayman	3	1
Jamaica	4	1
Guyana	3	1
Grenada	1	1
Canada	4	4
Ireland	4	–
New Zealand	4	4
India	3	2
Pakistan	4	1
Sri Lanka	4	1
Singapore	1	1

had met less than 10 times, about nine per cent of the respondents said that their committee had met between 10 and 24 times, while in the other three cases the respondents said that their committee had met between 25 and 49 times.

Key questions include: "Does the amount of activity relate to the PACs' characteristics?", "Is the productivity of PACs enhanced when they are chaired by an opposition MP?", "Does the presence of a larger contingent of opposition MPs make PACs more active?", and "Does the presence of a larger staff result in greater PAC output?"

We investigate each of these questions by performing two sets of analyses. First, we perform correlation analyses to see whether there is any association between the variables of interest. We then perform regression analyses to detect whether and to what extent the independent variables of interest (opposition Chair, number of opposition MPs serving on the committee and the size of the staff) have a

Table 8.3 Correlations. Determinants of activity (sig.)

Type of activity	Committee chaired by a member of the opposition	Number of opposition MPs serving on the PAC	Number of members of staff
Number of meetings	−.141	.577	.339
	(.530)	(.005)	(.123)
Number of reports	−.090	.416	.324
	(.104)	(.061)	(.152)

positive and statistically significant impact on the amount of activity carried out by the PAC, even when we control for the effects of other independent variables.

The results of the correlation analyses, presented in table 8.3, reveal that, contrary to what previous studies had assumed, the activity of a PAC is not enhanced by the Chairperson being from the opposition. The correlation coefficients are in fact negative and statistically insignificant. The correlation analysis also reveals that while the relationship between the number of staff members working for the committee is positively related to the amount of activity performed by the PAC, both in terms of hearings and reports, the coefficient is not significant. While the number of opposition MPs is positively related to both indicators of activity and, in one case, significantly so.

When we perform the regression analyses, we find that the impact of the number of opposition MPs on the number of hearings remains significant when we control for a whole range of other independent variables. In other words, the regression models reveal that PACs that have more opposition MPs among their members hold more meetings than those PACs in which there is a smaller contingent of opposition MPs. All the other control variables are instead statistically insignificant. (See table 8.4).

When we use instead the number of reports as our indicator of PAC's activity, we find slightly different results. While the number of opposition MPs serving on the committee was a major determinant of the number of meetings a PAC holds, it has no significant impact. Furthermore, while the number of staff members and the control variables for three regions included in the survey had no significant impact on the number of hearings, they had a significant impact on the number of reports. In fact, while the presence of a larger staff is

Table 8.4 Regression analysis. The determinants of the number of meetings (sig.)

	Model 1	Model 2
Intercept	1.843	2.699
	(.006)	(.009)
Opposition chair	−.855	.832
	(.136)	(.196)
Size of the committee		
Number of opposition	.296	.245
MPs in the PAC	(.004)	(.026)
Number of staffers	.053	.060
	(.218)	(.246)
Asia		−1.036
		(.270)
Caribbean		−.966
		(.259)
Africa		−.443
		(.566)
R−squared	.461	.531

conducive to the drafting of more PAC reports, the fact that a PAC operated in an Asian, African or Caribbean country depresses the production of committee reports.

The 2002 survey asked respondents to indicate not only how important they regarded certain conditions for the successful performance of a PAC, but it also asked them to indicate the frequency

Table 8.5 Regression analysis. The determinants of the number of reports (sig.)

	Model 1	Model 2
Intercept	1.082	3.412
	(.104)	(.000)
Opposition chair	−.498	−.402
	(.461)	(.380)
Size of the committee		
Number of opposition	.182	.069
MPs in the PAC	(.076)	(.344)
Number of staffers	.052	.088
	(.261)	(.024)
Asia		−3.146
		(.001)
Caribbean		−2.424
		(.003)
Africa		−1.587
		(.025)
R−squared	.267	.733

with which some results were achieved in the wake of the PAC's work – results that were regarded as important for keeping governments accountable for the expenditures of public money. While several studies (Stapenhurst *et al.*, 2005; Pelizzo *et al.*, 2006; Pelizzo and Stapenhurst, 2007) have analysed the perceived importance of the formal powers, composition and committee practices for the successful performance of the PAC, no study, to the best of our knowledge, has investigated the frequency with which certain results are achieved or the relationship between the amount of activities performed by the PACs and their ability to achieve certain goals.

The goals that were listed in the 2002 survey were: the frequency with which the government responds favourably to the recommendations formulated by the PAC, the frequency with which it implements the recommendations formulated by the PACs in their reports, the frequency with which legislation was modified in the wake of the committee's work, the frequency with which the integrity of the information provided by the government was improved as a consequence of the committee work, the frequency with which legal action was taken against officials who had violated the law and the frequency with which disciplinary action was taken against officials who had violated administrative guidelines. The data for the six indicators of PAC performance are presented in table 8.6.

The frequency with which these six results are achieved varies considerably. While a majority of respondents reported that the government responded favourably to the PACs recommendation and that it also improved the integrity of the information, a majority of respondents reported that legal action was taken and legislation was modified only seldomly. There is also considerable variation with regard to the number of cases in which an outcome is never achieved. PAC's recommendations are never implemented only in 4.8 per cent of the cases, legislation is never changed only in 5.3 per cent of the cases, the quality of information is never improved in 9.5 per cent of the cases, the government never responds favourably to the PACs' recommendation in 9.5 per cent of the cases, disciplinary action is never taken in 36.8 per cent of the cases, and legal action is never taken in 42.1 per cent of the cases.

Is the frequency with which each of these results is achieved related and possibly caused by the amount of activities performed by PACs? In order to test whether this is the case, we run two models for each of the outcomes variables (responds, implements, changes legislation,

Table 8.6 Measures of success: frequency with which certain results are achieved

Country	Govt. responds favourably to Committee recommendations	Govt. implements Committee recommendations	Changes in legislation were adopted as a result of Committee work	Improvements in the integrity of govt. information or databases	Legal action	Disciplinary action
Botswana	1	1	–	1	2	2
Gambia	2	2	1	1	1	–
Ghana	1	1	1	0	0	2
Kenya	1	1	1	1	1	1
Mozambique	1	1	2	2	0	0
Namibia	1	1	1	1	0	0
Nigeria	0	1	–	1	0	0
South Africa	2	2	2	2	1	1
Tanzania	1	1	1	1	1	1
Zambia	2	1	1	2	1	1
Anguilla	–	–	–	–	–	0
Barbados	1	1	1	1	1	1
Belize	–	–	–	–	–	–
Cayman	2	2	1	1	0	1
Jamaica	2	2	2	2	2	2
Guyana	–	–	–	–	0	0
Grenada	0	0	0	0	0	–
Canada	2	2	1	2	0	0
Ireland	2	2	2	2	1	1
New Zealand	2	2	1	2	0	0
India	2	2	2	2	1	2
Pakistan	2	2	2	2	1	2
Sri Lanka	2	1	1	2	–	–
Singapore	2	2	–	2	–	–

improves the integrity of information and so on). In the first model, we regress the dependent variable against the indicators of PACs' activity, namely the number of meetings held by the PAC and the number drafted by the PACs. In the second model, we regress the dependent variables against the indicators of PACs' activity while controlling for the effects of regional factors.

By performing these analyses we find that the second model, which includes the dummy variables for the Asian, African and Caribbean regions, explains a greater portion of the variance than the first model. More importantly, we find that, with only one exception, no regression coefficient has a statistically significant impact on our dependent variables. Only the number of reports significantly affects the frequency with which disciplinary action is taken against officials who violated administrative guidelines. But once we control for the impact of regional trends, even this coefficient becomes statistically insignificant.

While these analyses do not provide a proper explanation for the variation in the frequency with which various policy outcomes are actually achieved, it provides fairly conclusive evidence of the fact that the PACs' ability to achieve their policy goals has little if anything to do with the amount of activities PACs perform. Hence, the evidence sustains *prima facie* the claim that since there is no detectable (by quantitative analyses at least) relation between outputs and outcomes and it is inappropriate to assess the performance of an institutional body on the basis of the outputs it produces.

There is one additional point that has to be addressed. The literature has consistently noted that certain factors such as the size of the committee, the fact that the Chair of the PAC belongs to the opposition or the fact that a PAC is well staffed are crucial for the success of a PAC. In the previous section, we performed some analyses to test whether there is any detectable relationship between some structural features of a PAC and the amount of activity it performs. Do structural conditions affect the PAC's ability to achieve its goals and improve its performance?

To test whether this is indeed the case, we perform some regression analyses. For each of the important policy goals we run two different models. In the first model, we regress our dependent variable against three of the structural conditions that the literature regards as important, namely the presence of an opposition Chair, the number of opposition MPs and the size of the staff supporting the PAC. In

Table 8.7 PAC Activity and Success

The government	Intercept	Number of meetings	Number of reports	Asia	Caribbean	Africa	r-squared
Responds	1.111	.112	-.036				.028
	(.043)	(.524)	(.827)				
	1.857	.070	-.038	-.036	-.778	-1.006	.437
	(.054)	(.644)	(.847)	(.962)	(.327)	(.110)	
Implements	1.059	.038	.109				.072
	(.025)	(.797)	(.439)				
	1.345	.001	.163	.198	-.261	-.589	.355
	(.126)	(.993)	(.390)	(.776)	(.720)	(.299)	
Changes Legislation	.633	.172	.018				.092
	(.277)	(.343)	(.895)				
	-.253	.106	.207	1.255	.755	.672	.322
	(.801)	(.574)	(.297)	(.113)	(.334)	(.247)	
Improves the information it provides	.920	.068	.239				.097
	(.077)	(.685)	(.407)				
	1.066	.020	.213	.607	-.335	-.484	.487
	(.227)	(.889)	(276)	(.403)	(.654)	(.402)	
Legal action	1.34	-.077	-.234				.237
	(.025)	(.695)	(.159)				
	1.259	-.092	-.223	.397	-.034	.152	.273
	(.276)	(.670)	(.380)	(.682)	(.971)	(.831)	
Disciplinary action	.982	.250	-.433				.297
	(.084)	(.208)	(.029)				
	.940	.162	-.397	1.089	-.131	.322	.481
	(.399)	(.413)	(.122)	(.267)	(.886)	(.654)	

the second model, we regress our dependent variable against structural conditions controlling for regional effects. The results of our analyses are presented in table 8.8.

The statistical analyses presented in table 8.8 suggest three basic considerations. First of all, they suggest that with only one exception (changes in legislation), the explanatory power of the models is greatly improved when in addition to regress each of our dependent variables against the structural conditions variables we also control for the effects of the regional factors. In fact, the only coefficient that achieves statistical significance is the dummy variable for the Asian region presented in the last row of table 8.8. The second consideration is that while we found that some structural conditions affect the output of a PAC either in terms of the number of meetings held or in terms of the number of reports drafted by the committee, none of the structural conditions has a significant impact on the PAC's ability to achieve its policy goals. With this caveat in mind, namely that no structural condition variable is a statistically significant determinant of any of the policy goals, it is worth noting that the relationship to the impact of the presence of an opposition Chair varies across the various dependent variables. In fact, while the presence of an opposition Chair was negatively related to or, worse, had a negative impact on the amount of activity performed by a PAC and the frequency with which a PAC is able to get a favourable response from the government, to get its recommendations implemented, to have legislation modified or to have information improved, the presence of an opposition Chairperson is positively related or possibly has a positive influence on the frequency with which disciplinary and legal action are taken in the wake of a PAC's work.

There are two possible interpretations of this finding. The first is quite simply that that the presence of an opposition Chairperson improves a PAC's ability to achieve certain results and not others. In other words, there is a trade off in terms of what a PAC can accomplish with an opposition Chairperson. With an opposition Chairperson a PAC meets less frequently, writes fewer reports, and is less likely to get a favourable government response to the recommendations it formulates, to get said recommendations implemented, to force the government to modify legislation or to force the government to improve the quality of the information it provides. So if these are the policy outcomes that one regards as desirable, it is better not to have an opposition Chairperson. Conversely, if one believes that the importance of

Table 8.8 PAC Organisation and Success of PAC (sig.)

The government	intercept	Opposition chair	Opposition MPs	Size of staff	Asia	Caribbean	Africa	r-sq.
Responds	1.606 (.000)	-.556 (.165)	.046 (.495)	.005 (.872)				.121
	2.057 (.003)	-.199 (.609)	.020 (.758)	.015 (.612)	.099 (.858)	-.723 (.189)	-.797 (.101)	.399
Implements	1.614 (.000)	-.591 (.077)	.020 (.714)	.025 (.289)				.227
	2.231 (.000)	-.378 (.254)	-.010 (.850)	.024 (.351)	-.479 (.310)	-.685 (.139)	-.851 (.041)	.452
Changes Legislation	-1.065 (.019)	-.345 (.296)	.050 (.399)	.037 (.116)				.245
	-1.159 (.086)	-.327 (.398)	.041 (.572)	.032 (.344)	.062 (.917)	-.129 (.807)	-.022 (.960)	.252
Improves the information it provides	1.598 (.001)	-.516 (.178)	.011 (.862)	.036 (.197)				.189
	2.243 (.001)	-.230 (.547)	-.024 (.701)	.020 (.509)	-.205 (.706)	-.992 (.074)	-.785 (.099)	.425
Legal action	.588 (.243)	.605 (.138)	-.086 (.230)	.014 (.619)				.210
	.537 (.451)	.801 (.100)	-.094 (.249)	-.030 (.537)	1.150 (.240)	.050 (.934)	.069 (.891)	.317
Disciplinary action	.298 (.609)	.159 (.740)	.058 (.468)	.033 (.336)				.115
	-.252 (.737)	.387 (.429)	.073 (.378)	-.043 (.415)	2.371 (.036)	.532 (.419)	.623 (.266)	.406

having disciplinary and legal action taken in the wake of PAC work exceeds the importance of having more meetings or more reports, then one has to regard the presence of an opposition MP as highly preferable.

While the previous interpretation treats the various policy goals as relatively homogenous, the second interpretation is based instead on the realisation that the policy goals that we have discussed so far are very different from one another. The first four (the government responds, implements, changes legislation or provides better information) pertain to the sphere of executive-legislative relationships, to the parliament's ability to adequately perform its oversight function and to keep the government accountable for its actions. The other two policy goals concern instead events that go beyond the realm of executive-legislative relations. Hence, once we acknowledge that the policy goals that we have so far discussed differ from one another not only in degree (one policy goal is more important than another), but also in kind, we are in a better position to understand the meaning of our statistical analyses. The data indicate that while the PAC's ability to perform its normal oversight functions is not enhanced by the presence of an opposition Chairperson, an opposition Chair may be quite instrumental in ensuring that proper disciplinary or legal action, that goes beyond normal committee work, is taken in the wake of the committee work.[10]

So while the data sustain the claim that structural features may be conditionally relevant, they do not support the claim that the successful performance of a PAC stems necessarily from the way it is organised.

This point can be illustrated not only on the basis of quantitative data but also on the basis of qualitative data. In fact, if performance were a function of organisational features alone, PACs with similar structural and organisational characteristics should perform similarly. Yet, this is far from being the case. Studies conducted on the PACs of the Pacific Island States (Rawlings, 2006; Pelizzo, 2010b) have shown that while the PAC from the Solomon Islands and that of Vanuatu had similar structural characteristics, they were respectively one the best and one of the worst performing PACs in the region.

Section four: PAC performance and the strategic interaction model

The data presented above downsized the importance that previous studies had assigned to the institutionalisation, structure, organisation, leadership, partisan composition and formal powers of PACs.

The variables previously regarded as the most important determinants of PAC performance are only conditionally relevant; that is, they are relevant only provided that they are put to some good use. In other words, for oversight to be effective, the oversight potential or capacity has to be used in practice. But while greater or lesser oversight capacity may affect the effectiveness of oversight activity, the availability of oversight tools is by itself insufficient to ensure that such tools will be employed effectively.

The decision to use or not to use oversight tools, to perform or not to perform an oversight activity, is a decision that has to be explained in agential and not structural terms. It requires a micro-level not a macro-level explanation.

This is precisely the kind of explanation that is provided by the strategic interaction model presented in Chapter 7. The model makes it clear that in the wake of a legitimacy crisis, if the population and civil society groups are not satisfied by the ruling elite's response to their demands, they can place the ruling elite before two options: either becoming irresponsive to voter demands at the risk of more widespread social discontent or making the newly established institutions work effectively.

This explanation is superior to previous explanations for a variety of reasons: it explains an agential choice that macro-level explanations, by design, are ill-equipped to grasp; it does so by combining explanatory variables that had previously been used in isolation. For example, while Rawlings (2006) understood the importance of agential, voluntaristic elements in explaining the performance of PACs, his analyses had a somewhat fatalistic undertone: his position was that if there is political will, PACs will work well; if there is no such will, PACs will not work well or, perhaps, not at all.

Such an approach was problematic not only for its unspoken fatalism, but also for its static understanding of political will. Yet, as Skocpol (2003) had made clear, while interactions between social groups are to some extent path-dependent and are embedded in long-established social understandings and roles, they are, at the same time, very dynamic in the sense that actors may change preferences, choices and strategies in response to the behaviour of their counterparts. This is a fairly useful insight for it provides a theoretical rationale for merging the voluntaristic arguments presented by Rawlings (2006) with the demand for good governance arguments that Pelizzo and Stapenhurst had discussed in several of their works.

The strategic interaction model, presented in Chapter 7, formalises a dynamic interaction between social demands on the one hand and political will on the other hand. By developing this strategic interaction model, we go beyond our previous work in that we are able to suggest why the demand for good governance matters, as Rawlings (2006) had already done, but at the same time we are able to go beyond Rawlings for we show how this political will can be induced. Furthermore, while we acknowledge the importance of popular demands and the media (Pelizzo and Stapenhurst, 2007), we go further and show how popular demands and media contribute to creating and sustaining the will to change. By being able to show why and when PACs' formal powers may be used, we are able to show that structural and macro-level factors matter conditionally if and when they are put to good use. By doing so we are able to go beyond the studies that have a macro-level focus, since we are able to answer a question that escapes their theoretical horizon, namely why actors sometimes use certain oversight tools and some other times they do not.

We have claimed that our strategic interaction model works for explaining both the adoption of and the performance of PACs. With regard to the adoption of PACs (as for other governance reforms) we have claimed that they amount to responses to crises and critical events such as corruption and loss of legitimacy. Since newly established PACs are found in countries with various levels of good governance, the reader may be somewhat perplexed by our statements. A few words of clarification may be in order.

The political system, the political elite, in order to regain voter trust, to regain legitimacy, to legitimise itself, to safeguard itself and the political system in which it operates, proposes and adopts institutional reforms not only to fix real or perceived problems but also to signal to the voters their commitment to making the political system work better. This basic lesson, we believe, can be applied to any kind of political reform: from the constitutional reform that aims to increase government effectiveness (France V Republic) to the electoral reform that aims to create a more direct linkage between electors and elected (Italy, 1993 electoral reforms); from the adoption of a PAC to oversee government spending (Indonesia, 2009) to the reform of the National Audit Office in Finland.[11]

Does our strategic interaction model also explain performance? We believe so, as we will now demonstrate.

PAC performance in Pacific Island States

The parliaments of Vanuatu, Kiribati and the Solomon Islands all have PACs. The PAC in the Solomon Islands operates under the dispositions of the parliament's standing orders (art. 69), it operates under the Expenditure Review and Audit act in Vanuatu, and it operates under a wider set of normative dispositions in Kiribati where the existence, role and function of the PAC is recognised in the Constitution (art. 115) and in the parliament's Standing Orders.

If we assess the effectiveness of PAC performance on the basis of the timeliness of PAC report, the above-mentioned Pacific Island States display considerable variation. In fact, while the examination of the reports of the Auditor General is usually completed within three months in Samoa, it may take up to a year in the Solomon Islands, more than a year in Kiribati and even longer in Vanuatu.[12]

Similarly, in Kiribati the PAC reports on government accounts and the audits of the Auditor General (AG) are not timely either. The delay with which the accounts of the government, statutory bodies and companies are presented does not allow the AG to report in a timely fashion, which in turn prevents the PAC from reporting to parliament and parliament debating the PAC reports in a timely manner. For instance, the AG report on the Government accounts for the year 2004, submitted with a two-year delay, were debated in parliament in the first quarter of 2008. Several observers in the international community have noted that the delay with which the government now submits its accounts to the office of the AG is much less than it used to be, and there has been no improvement in how timely statutory bodies and companies are in submitting the accounts. The un-timeliness of the reports has major consequences. One report on *Good Leadership* in Kiribati lamented that:

> The backlog of accounts from Government, statutory bodies and companies, which were often presented for auditing several years after the end of the financial year, did not allow for the Auditor-General to report on Government accounts in a timely manner. As such, his report was often several years late, and would often pass without the scrutiny of the *Maneaba ni Maungatabu*.
>
> (p.41)

In contrast to the ineffectiveness of the PAC in Kiribati and Vanuatu, the PAC of Samoa and the Solomon Islands are remarkably more effective. In Samoa, the PAC operates in a very timely manner and is regarded to be one of the most effective PACs in the region. In the Solomon Islands, the performance of the PAC is not as timely as that of its Samoan counterpart. As the PEFA report pointed out, while the PAC in the Solomon Islands had become increasingly more effective in performing its tasks in the 2006–7 period, its timeliness and effectiveness has been significantly reduced in the following period by a government crisis, the death of the AG and so on. Yet, in spite of these difficulties, the timeliness in operations sustains the claim that the PAC from the Solomon Islands operates more effectively than its counterpart in Kiribati.

This conclusion is further corroborated by additional evidence. In Kiribati, the problems that were denounced in earlier AG reports are again criticised in more recent reports, very few of the PAC recommendations are acted upon, the PAC has very little capacity to follow up on its recommendations and there seems to be very little interest in recovering misallocated money. To quote, once again, the report on *Good Leadership*, there is little improvement in how the PAC functions:

> This is evidenced by the fact that the same findings recur annually, the failure to respond to Audit queries is not considered as constituting serious misconduct; and there is a significant lack of urgency to recover lost funds and stores (totalling $361,826.98 as at end of 2007) and a failure to prosecute public servants for fraud, embezzlement or misappropriation.
>
> (p. 51)

By contrast, in the Solomon Islands the actions of the AG and of the PAC indicate that there is and there has been a sense of urgency in recovering lost funds and misallocated moneys. In a span of a few days in October, the Auditor General made the headlines on a daily basis: on 14 October 2008, the AG found that $200,000 in aid fund had been misused and that $2 million had "not be [sic] properly accounted for"; on 15 October, the AG denounced that $3.5 million, allocated for the reforestation project, had not been properly used and that "a significant sum of money has been illegally expended", that a former minister had not repaid a $27 thousand *per diem* he had received, that an imprest of $189,000 that should have been retired by 31 September 2007 had not been retired, and that there had been irregularities in the sale of 130 government properties, and so on.[13] Coupled with an energetic AG, the PAC of the Solomon Islands has been one of the most successful PACs in the Asia-Pacific region and was praised by the Solomon Islands' chapter of Transparency International.

If we take the sense of urgency mentioned in the report as an indication of the political will to promote good governance, we have already provided some empirical evidence to support our strategic interaction model: whether institutional reforms occur and whether the good governance institutions work effectively, it is a matter of political will.

The evidence from the Pacific Island States allows us to provide some empirical support for the last piece of our model, namely that the political will to make newly established reforms work effectively is not spontaneous, it is not self-generating, it is not always sincere. The will to make these institutions work effectively may be induced by popular pressure/demands and by the media. The case of the Solomon Islands is emblematic in this respect.[14] The articles published in the *Solomon Star* leave no doubt as to the fact that the media and a vast segment of the population have a very strong stance against corruption. Take, for example, an unsigned political editorial published by the *Solomon Star* on 8 November 2008. The author of this article, after underlining that we all know that "politicians interfere with government budgets", that "they want to have a hand in almost everything to do with money", that they want to "have their way around … legal or illegal", went on to say that "the Public Account Committee is closely examining why public funds are being abused and what should be done about it" and then concluded that "we hope they'll come up with new measures to put an end to this corruption". The fact that the media have launched a crusade against corruption, that they shame politicians involved in less than licit deals, that they praise politicians involved in the fight against corruption, makes it worthwhile for MPs serving on the PACs to take their committee duties seriously.

To sum up our evidence: the media shame and blame, the voters become concerned with the behaviour of politicians and institutions, popular and media demands/pressure induce in the political class a will to act, and this is how we end up having institutions that work effectively – as our strategic interaction model has posited.

Conclusions

In this chapter, we tested our theoretical model presented in Chapter 7, using empirical data collected in two surveys of PACs undertaken by WBI in 2002 and 2008–9. We used these data to show that earlier explanations developed by scholars do not provide convincing explanations for why PACs work effectively. In contrast to scholars who had argued that PAC performance reflects the size, the formal powers, the partisan composition, the institutionalisation, the partisan affiliation of the Chairperson, our analyses revealed that none of these factors matters much and understandably so: if these factors are fixed, and they are fixed, they cannot account for within-country variation over time. They can at best be used to explain cross-country variation.

The problem we are confronted with is, Why do we detect variation over time in how a PAC performs? This problem that can only be explained by abandoning a static, macro-level focus and adopting a micro approach, such as the one we presented in Chapter 7. The evidence generated from the Pacific Island States illustrates quite clearly how well our model works out in explaining PAC performance.

And finally, it is important for scholars working on PACs, for we believe that our strategic interaction model addresses a set of variables, issues and problems that the PAC literature, with its macro focus, had so far been unable to tackle. So, to various extents, we believe that this study contributes to three literatures.

This said, we believe that the main claim to fame of this work is its policy relevance. In fact, our model and our findings have clear behavioural implications in that they set out very clearly what the international community, international organisations and practitioners should do to promote democracy, high democratic quality and good governance. To promote good governance, effective oversight must be secured, and the only way to ensure that oversight activities are performed effectively is to create a popular demand for effective oversight – a demand that has to come from society and has to be sustained by the media.

9 Conclusions

Our objective in this book has been to present a new theory of legislative oversight. The main claim of our strategic interaction model is that in order to know whether legislative oversight is performed effectively we need to know the strategic interaction between (members of) the ruling elite and society. In fact, we suggested that ruling elites introduce and implement institutional reforms and use effectively the newly established/adopted institutional devices if, in the wake of a legitimacy crisis, there is a popular demand for change. We also noted that this demand has to be sustained over time because, otherwise, the ruling elite may adopt new institutional devices but not feel compelled to use them effectively. In detailing our theory, our strategic interaction model, we underlined that it involves several elements and actors: a legitimacy crisis, a ruling elite, society with its demands and the media. Specifically, we noted that the media play a key role in sustaining voter demands for institutional change and performance and, consequently, ensure that reforms adopted to improve the quality of democracy or the level of good governance will deliver the expected results. The conclusions presented in this chapter strengthen our theoretical claims in three ways.

First, this chapter revisits the main claims formulated in the previous chapters, namely that:

- quality of democracy and the level of corruption are affected by effective oversight
- that effective oversight is not a necessary nor an automatic consequence of oversight capacity
- that agency theory is essential in understanding why oversight tools or capacity are used in some instances but not in others

- and that our strategic interaction model provides a fairly good explanation for why governance reforms are sometimes undertaken and
- for why, under some circumstances, tools designed to promote reduced corruption and/or enhanced quality of democracy are used effectively.

Second, this chapter explores some of the possible implications of our findings, not only for the study of legislative oversight, but also, and more importantly, for the promotion of good governance and higher democratic quality/qualities in countries that are not usually regarded as the most obvious basket cases of democratic quality or good governance.

Finally, our theory stresses the importance of the role that free media can play not only to make democracy in its most minimalist form exist, but also to ensure that democracy works well and is of a higher quality by helping prevent corruption, as well as minimising misconduct and other forms of illicit and/or unethical behaviour. Specifically, we argue that the media makes voters aware of the importance of good governance and stresses that good governance may contribute to a better functioning of the political system. This in turn may help minimise misallocation of resources and create the conditions for sustainable economic growth, development and poverty alleviation, thereby generating and sustaining popular demand for good governance. This is precisely what is required to ensure the adoption and the effective use of oversight tools.

This chapter comprises four sections. First, we reconsider oversight, democracy and good governance, then we present some implications for the international community. We briefly consider the application of our model in highly fragmented societies. We conclude by presenting three lessons.

Section one: oversight, democracy and good governance

We begin by restating an important point: the international community has, for the past two decades, advanced two different, albeit related, claims: that legislative oversight is good for democracy (and the quality thereof) and that legislative oversight is beneficial for good governance, or at least a key element of good governance, namely the control of corruption. We could, of course, comment on how democracy and good governance are conceptualised, how they cover more or less extensive portions of the semantic field and how they can be viewed as completely distinct entities, as partially overlapping or as coinciding notions. We could also reiterate what Sartori (1976) as well as several semioticians have noted, namely that there is a trade off between the intension and the extension of a concept. In other words, the more narrowly we define a concept, the more precise its meaning, whereas the more extensively we define a concept, the less precise its meaning. Important as these semiotic issues are, they are not the main focus of the present analysis. What matters, for our purposes, is that regardless of how poorly/well and imprecisely/precisely the international community understands and defines democracy and good governance (or corruption control), it firmly believes that they are both a function of legislative oversight.

Specifically, the international community holds the belief that corruption control/democracy stems directly and necessarily from effective oversight which, in its turn, is a simple function of the oversight capacity at the disposal of a given legislature.

This understanding had major practical implications. If effective oversight is a function of legislative oversight capacity, if legislative oversight capacity is simply the sum of the oversight tools at the disposal of a legislature, if a legislature adopts more oversight tools, then it would be a more effective overseer of government activities and will make democracy work better. It will increase the level of corruption control, and, by doing so, will secure higher rates of sustainable economic growth and socio-economic development.

One could of course argue that our account is not just a stylised account, but that it is an inaccurate one. For instance, one could say that some studies conducted under the aegis of international organisations have stressed the importance of contextual factors, have stressed the fact that sometimes legislatures are so corrupt that they cannot even be thought of as having the slightest interest in overseeing the executive or curbing corruption. But while these arguments seem to contradict our stylised account of how the international community understands the oversight-democracy-good governance nexus, they actually do not contradict us at all. Quite the opposite. Having recognised that legislatures are sometimes partially responsible for the low level of good governance that one finds in a given country, international organisations have at times advocated the adoption of legislative codes of conduct. By adopting a code of conduct, a legislature takes care of its own internal problem, it curbs and possibly eliminates the misconduct of its members, it becomes an agent of good governance, oversees the executive and makes democracy work better – exactly as we noted in our stylised account.

The argument of the contextualists, as summarised by Wang (2005), also fails to refute our account: the Wang model simply posits that oversight capacity works better under specific contextual conditions, as we have discussed earlier on. But once we know that any two countries have the same context, oversight is performed more effectively in the country where the legislature has a greater arsenal of oversight tools, because, even Wang believes, in spite of superficial attention to the context in which political actors operate, all the variance in oversight effectiveness is the product of fixed, structural, institutional conditions. Yet, as Stapenhurst (2011) made clear, if we only focus on structural conditions, we explain only a fairly modest portion in the variance of oversight effectiveness and in legislatures' ability, through an effective oversight activity, to improve the quality of democracy and corruption control. And the reason why structural conditions can only explain a (small) portion of legislative effectiveness is that by focusing on oversight capacity alone, on the presence/absence of oversight tools, the explanation provides very little indication of whether, why and under what circumstances these oversight tools are actually used. Not surprisingly, in our analyses of the relationship between oversight on the one hand and democracy and corruption control on the other hand, we found that while democracy and corruption control are both significantly affected by oversight effectiveness, they are virtually insensitive to changes in oversight capacity – both because oversight capacity has little to explain in addition to what is already explained by oversight effectiveness and also because oversight capacity contributes little to oversight effectiveness.

In the light of this empirical evidence, we suggest two conclusions: that while international organisations were correct in understanding the role legislative oversight may play in improving the quality of democracy or the control of corruption, they made a mistake in assuming that oversight effectiveness and oversight capacity could be treated as one and the same thing; that in order to understand what makes oversight effective, we need to bring agency back into the analytical framework of legislative oversight.

Our strategic interaction model is precisely an attempt to do so, by highlighting that the ruling elite will adopt some good governance reforms and will use the newly adopted oversight tools effectively only if there is a sustained demand for good governance. Where there is no demand for good governance, no reform will be carried out; where an initial demand for good governance quickly fades, institutional reforms may be made but the newly created institutions are not used effectively. Conversely, where there is a sustained demand, reforms are adopted and effectively implemented.

In doing so, the analytical framework we have devised refines the conventional wisdom in three respects: first, it shows that oversight effectiveness cannot be explained exclusively by macro-level variables and that we need to understand the role of agency. Second, it makes it clear how important demands are in the political system. While there is no doubt that that parties sometimes neglect voter demands, it is also clear that they cannot afford to neglect voter demand all the time. Otherwise, the disgruntled voter, the voter who feels betrayed, dissatisfied, un-represented, will perceive the political system parties as a cartel and will cast his/her ballot for populist and anti-system parties and movements (Pelizzo, 2003). It is quite clear that when voters are dissatisfied with, for instance, the level of corruption in a political system, the ruling elite can either adopt some reform to regain citizen trust or can neglect voter demands and run the serious risk of being voted out of office. Third, our analysis makes clear that important as voter demands may be, they need to last over time to have some kind of impact on the functioning of the political system and we argue that the media play a key role in maintaining such demands. In the case of anti-corruption reforms, for example, in those polities where the media exposed instances of illicit behaviour, shamed the corrupt politicians and launched an attack against corruption, it helped sustain voter demands for reforms and was pivotal in securing that oversight tools were used effectively.

Section two: implications for the international community

In the previous section, we underlined what we regard as our main contributions to the study of legislative oversight in a comparative perspective – contributions that will, hopefully, force the structuralists to reconsider some of their ideas and bring to an end the erroneous habit of equating oversight effectiveness and capacity. But in spite of the intellectual merits of our insight, we believe that our analytical framework is even more significant for its practical implications.

For years, the international community has assumed that by expanding the oversight capacity of legislatures, by adopting new oversight tools, such as, for example, Public Accounts Committees (PACs), legislatures would perform their oversight tasks with greater effectiveness and would, by doing so, contribute to the promotion of good governance, reduce corruption and improve the quality of democracy. Our findings raise doubts as to whether all the good things go together. Our analyses indicate that oversight potential or capacity, that is, the arsenal of oversight tools at the disposal of a legislature, is neither a significant determinant of oversight effectiveness nor of democratic quality and not even of corruption control. Legislatures may be well equipped to oversee the executive, but if there is no political will to use such oversight tools, oversight will not be performed, or at least will not be performed effectively and will induce neither an improvement in democracy nor in the level of corruption.

The present study makes it clear that what matters in order to promote the good functioning of a democratic regime is oversight effectiveness, which, in its turn, is not a mere function of macro-level, structural, institutional conditions, but is instead a function of micro-level, agential factors such as the will to adopt and use oversight tools effectively.

The key contribution of the present study is to show that regardless of whether the ruling elite is reform-oriented or not and what its preferences are, it can always be induced to make some institutional reform, adopt oversight tools and use them effectively by a sustained popular demand. While a stream of party-politics theorising has emphasised the growing detachment of and a growing gap between the system parties and their respective electorates, in various policy realms (management of the economy, foreign policy, reform of the welfare state) we believe that system parties and governments can afford to ignore popular demands only when the political system is operating under what might be called "normal circumstances". But as we have made clear, when a legitimacy crisis occurs, system parties and governments can ignore popular demands only at the risk of being voted out of office and of being replaced by more extremist political parties and movements which may be associated with a more general system breakdown.

This is why, when popular demand for reforms emerges in the wake of a legitimacy crisis, the ruling elite cannot afford to neglect society's demands and is induced, more or less reluctantly, to adopt some institutional reforms. We also claim that the existence and the persistence of such reformist demand, that in the first instance is conducive to an institutional reform, can also lead to an effective use of the newly adopted institutional devices.

If the existence and persistence of popular demands are responsible for the institutional change and performance, the international community and international organisations have to modify their strategy. They need to abandon their focus on simply building legislative oversight capacity, that is, on the expansion of oversight tools, and focus instead on how a demand for enhanced democracy and governance can be stimulated and sustained.

In the past decade or so, the international community has run innumerable conferences, workshops and seminars for political elites. For the most part these activities covered similar themes and issues, namely to have more effective legislative oversight. Often, they presented the findings of studies on the factors associated with corruption and strengthened participants' understanding of the complexity and multi-causal nature of this phenomenon. The issues and themes were also, for the most part, fairly similar and covered notions of good governance and corruption, as well as a consideration of the role that parliament can play in fighting corruption and promoting good governance, the instruments of parliamentary oversight and the role of parliament in the budget process. Over time, new themes, such as codes of conduct for legislators, emerged and were integrated into program design, but the overall framework was never questioned and the idea that stronger legislatures are essential for keeping governments accountable was never challenged.

What was missing from this technocratic approach, which was largely addressed to parliamentarians and other members of the political elite, was an emphasis on securing popular demand by citizens for better governance. If there is a popular demand for governance reforms, the political elite comes under pressure and has an incentive to make some institutional reforms, the reformist process has a significant chance of succeeding and the reform-oriented politicians may enjoy some electoral success because of their reformist agenda.[1]

Popular demand for governance reforms cannot be generated solely by running workshops and seminars for the political elite. It is essential to explain to citizens – the voters – why they may benefit (in the not so long run) from greater oversight effectiveness, better governance and higher rates of growth. For as long as the population at large is not aware of the benefits associated with improvements in democracy and governance, it will neither support nor demand a departure from the status quo and will not create the conditions for institutional change and performance.

Section three: highly fragmented societies

In some ethnically fragmented polities, where the party system is so hyper-fragmented, fractionalised or atomised (Sartori, 1976) that one can wonder whether the party system can in fact be regarded as a party system at all, representatives can be elected in relatively small electoral districts with little more than a handful of votes. In polities of this kind, the elected MP has an incentive to reward his or her voters, to preserve their support and gain re-election. Meanwhile, voters have an incentive to support their vote-buying MP for the goods that he or she delivers to his/her supporters to significantly improve their standard of living, their material conditions and so on. Therefore, in these kinds of setting, neither the elected nor the electors have an incentive to depart from the status quo, abandon pork-barrel and/or vote-buying practices. Furthermore, in this kind of setting, if the media were to launch an anti-corruption campaign, they would fail to achieve substantive results, for they would not be able to secure popular support for the campaign itself.

To change this state of things, it is essential to persuade voters that if they abandon the vote of exchange and cast their ballot on other grounds, the loss of the benefits associated in the short term with the vote of exchange will be more than compensated with a vote cast on policy ground.[2] It is only when voters realise that casting their ballot for a vote-buying MP is not their most efficient utility-maximising strategy that they will consider abandoning the status quo, the vote of exchange, the political/electoral corruption and the misallocation of resources for a new and better system.

In other words, to create the conditions for institutional change and for the adoption of democratic and governance reforms, it is necessary to create a demand for good governance. This demand, in turn, can be created by highlighting the material benefits associated with a democracy of a higher level and with better levels of governance.

When a demand for enhanced democracy and good governance has emerged, the disclosure of illicit, illegal, unethical, corrupt practices is more likely to occur and to generate a legitimacy crisis for the ruling elite which, in turn, will have to accept the reformist process as the only way to safeguard its position and the survival of the whole political system.

While legitimacy crisis and popular demands are the main drivers of institutional change, the effectiveness of institutional performance depends on whether demands for good governance are sustained over time. In this respect, we observed that the media plays a key role in informing voters about the ethical/unethical behaviour of politicians, uncovering scandals, launching investigations and reportages, providing moral support and sometimes information to oversight agencies. This is why we believe that the media are, along with legitimacy crisis and popular demands, the third engine of our strategic interaction model.

Section four: some lessons?

In this book, we make several claims. We claim that effective oversight is good for the quality of democracy, that it is good for good governance and that international organisations were correct in hypothesising a beneficial relationship between effective oversight and good governance/democratic quality. However, we also claim that international organisations were less correct in equating oversight effectiveness with oversight capacity and that international organisations, and institutional and constitutional reformers should have paid greater attention to agential forces. This is precisely what we have attempted to do by developing our strategic interaction model. If we are correct in stating that agential factors play a greater role in promoting good governance than scholars and practitioners have so far been able/willing to acknowledge, we can propose three lessons.

The first lesson is that international organisations that have played a major role in disseminating knowledge as to the relationship between development, corruption and democracy, should learn to learn. In spite of the fact that a growing body of research had shown that the performance of oversight tools such as PACs was not significantly affected by structural, organisational and institutional features, international organisations keep emphasising the importance of these features. For example, in the case of PACs, international organisations stress the importance of Chairpersons belonging to opposition parties to securing PAC performance. Recent studies have shown that the partisan affiliation of the Chairperson has little to no impact on how the PAC functions. Hence, the first lesson is: learn to learn.

By learning to learn, international organisations may discover that in addition to focusing on structural, cultural, institutional and constitutional factors, they need to pay greater attention to agential factors. Structural and cultural factors change only slowly and over very long periods of time. Hence, in order to make an institutional change effective in a relatively short time span, it is necessary to focus on the incentives confronting the political class. If the ruling elite is confronted with legitimacy issues and popular demands for reform, it has to act quickly. In short, if international organisations wish to promote governance reforms in a speedy and efficient way, they need to focus on agential factors as well as on structural ones. Hence, the second lesson is: focus on agential factors.

Our third and final lesson is, it's all about demand. No change, institutional, constitutional or otherwise, will occur in the absence of a demand for such change. While social scientists tend to overlook or underestimate the importance of demand, it is one of the most powerful forces in the realm of social phenomena. This general principle also holds true with regard to governance reforms and institutional performance. Only if there is a popular demand for good governance will the ruling elite be compelled to depart from the status quo both formally and substantively. Hence, the third lesson is: ensure that there is a demand for democracy and governance. In the absence of such demand, reforms will not be adopted and institutions will not be used effectively.

We hope that by emphasising the importance of knowledge, agency and demand, we have not only corrected some of the previously held assumptions that were somewhat misleading, but that we have also provided some useful advice and guidance to scholars, practitioners and institutional reformers in achieving greater success in the years to come. We also hope that the research findings presented in this book trigger more and better research, without which no progress can be achieved.

Notes

1 Introduction

1 The expression that Kuhn (1962) used to describe scientific revolutions.
2 The most comprehensive work on the relationship between democracy and development was produced by Przeworski et al. (2000). Starting from the assumption that democracy is a regime that entails (i) uncertainty of the electoral outcome, (ii) the certainty that "whoever wins election will be allowed to assume office" (Przeworski et al., 2000: 17) and (iii) that electoral "outcomes are temporary" (Przeworski et al., 2000: 18) and that elections have to be held regularly, Przeworski and his colleagues set four rules to identify whether a regime is democratic or not: (i) the chief executive, president or prime minister, must be elected; (ii) the legislative branch of government must be elected; (iii) there must be multi-party competition; and (iv) there must be alternation in office. If one or more of these conditions is not met, a country cannot be regarded as democratic. The dataset developed by Przeworski et al. "covers 141 countries between 1950 (or year of independence) and 1990" (2000: 29). The author found that in this period there were 105 democracies and 133 dictatorships and "of the total 4730 years countries lived 1723 (36 percent) years under democracy and 3007 (64 percent) under dictatorship". Countries were treated as having non-democratic rule for violations of one or more of the above-listed rules. The statistical analyses performed to investigate the relationship between democracy and development were performed by using this dataset. Specifically, they tested whether development sparks transitions to democracy, whether development secures democratic consolidation and whether democracy promotes economic growth. This said, Przeworski et al. were quick to note that while development has little impact on the probability that a country becomes democratic, it has a major impact on whether a country is able to remain democratic. In fact, they noted that while a democratic regime has 12 per cent probability of collapsing in a given year in countries where the income per capita is less than US $1000, the probability is just 5.5 per cent in countries with an income per capita in the US $1000–2000 range and that in countries with a per capita income of more than US $5000 it is virtually impossible for democracy to break down. This evidence sustains Lipset's (1959) claim that the reason why democracies are more (likely to be) developed than non-democracies is that development is a major determinant of whether a democracy is able to

survive or not. Finally, Przeworski *et al.* (2000) tested whether democracy is a major determinant of economic growth. This was an important test for two different reasons. It was an important test because, as we have noted earlier on, several of Lipset's critics had criticised Lipset for not clarifying whether democracy was a cause or a consequence of development. Second, this test was also important because several studies (Huntington, 1968) had argued that the promotion of socio-economic development required strong government, strong states, strong political institution (what he called political development) rather than democracy and that development was more likely to be promoted by strong non-democratic governments than by feeble democratic ones. Hence, by testing whether democracy promotes growth Przeworski *et al.* (2000) could provide some empirical evidence to support or challenge the arguments advanced by Huntington (1968), Macridis (1968), Rustow (1968) and Weiner (1987). In this respect, Przeworski *et al.* (2000) found that growth is slightly higher under dictatorship than under democratic rule but that the finding is spurious in the sense that what makes a difference in terms of growth is not so much the regime type but rather "the conditions under which these regimes were observed" (2000: 147, 153 and 178). In other words, according to Przeworski *et al.* (2000), the fact that a political regime is democratic or not does not make much of a difference in terms of how fast a country's economy grows. This finding is important for two reasons. It is important because it shows that Huntington's claim that strong, authoritarian governments are better equipped than democratic ones to promote economic growth and development is not supported by empirical evidence and, therefore, there is not developmental justification for non-democratic rule. Development can occur under democracy just as well as it may occur under dictatorship. Second, and contra the modernisation theorists, this finding illustrates that the reason why democracies are disproportionately more developed than non democratic regime is not due to the fact that democracies experience higher growth rates than dictatorships but is due instead to the fact that economically developed democracies survive longer.

3 These views represented the received wisdom until 1968 when Huntington published *Political Order in Changing Societies*, in which he argued that development and rapid development are a destabilising force and could cause the breakdown of young, and poorly institutionalised democracies.

4 An additional criticism to Lipset's work, but in more general terms to both Marxist and liberal historiography, was developed by Rueschemeyer, Stephens and Stephens (1992). These authors contend that while it is true that socio-economic development created the conditions for the expansion and the political empowerment of the middle class or bourgeoisie, it neglects entirely the role of the working class in the process of democratic consolidation. Worse, this approach neglects entirely the fact that while the middle classes were pro-democratic in some instances, that is, whenever they were trying to downsize the political power of monarchs and aristocrats, they were also anti-democratic forces in all those instances in which they felt that their interests were threatened by democracy. Contra Lipset (1959), Rueschemeyer, Stephens and Stephens (1992: 57) suggest that democracy is not the product of the expansion and the empowerment of the middle classes, but of the working class and of the other lower, under-privileged classes because "those who have only to gain from democracy will be its most reliable promoters and

defenders", while the members of the middle and upper classes are those who will be "most tempted to roll it back when the occasion presents itself" (1992: 57). After positing the centrality of the role of the (working) class in securing the successful transition and consolidation of democracy, Rueschemeyer, Stephens and Stephens (1992) went on to argue that socio-economic development created the conditions for the political activation of the working class and of the other under-privileged classes. The advance by democracy was made possible by "the size and the density of organization of the working class" and this, in its turn, had been expanded by the transformation of the economic system from one that was mostly agricultural to one that was mostly industrial. This transformation not only expanded the number of urban workers but it also created the conditions for the emergence of workers' organisations and collective action. Regardless of whether development creates the condition for the establishment and the consolidation of democracy because it empowers the middle classes (Lipset) or the lower classes (Rueschemeyer, Stephens and Stephens), both analytical frameworks agree, though for different reasons, on the relationship between democracy and development – which is all the Lipset Hypothesis ultimately posits.

5 There is no consensus in the literature on the definition of legislative oversight (Olson, 2008) and, like the broader field of legislative studies, the concept is under-theorised. There are few global analyses.

6 Most analyses are undertaken at a country or regional level, often within a loose theoretical framework (e.g., Olson and Norton, 1996; Norton and Ahmed, 1999). These studies typically examine legislative functions within countries more generally, and do not focus solely, or particularly, on oversight. Furthermore, while there is a plethora of studies on the oversight function in the United States, there are only a relatively small number of studies outside the United States.

7 However, Rockman (1984) and Ogul and Rockman (1990) noted that there is much greater variety as to how oversight can be defined, and that definitions of oversight range from minimalistic to all-encompassing.

2 Theoretical foundations of legislative oversight

1 The principal of which are Gerring and Thacker (2004), Lederman *et al.*, (2005), Doig and Theobald (2000), Hope (2000), Persson *et al.* (1997) and Treisman (2000).

2 However, Rockman (1984) and Ogul and Rockman (1990) noted that there is much greater variety as to how oversight can be defined, and that definitions of oversight range from minimalistic to all-encompassing.

3 See n. 1, Chapter 3.

4 Strom (2000) usefully suggests that *principal-agent theory* is related to *delegation*. He argues that, because it is not possible to trust people to whom one delegates (e.g. politicians), delegation needs to be coupled with some mechanisms of *accountability*. Strom argues that, in its ideal form parliamentary democracy is a chain of delegation and accountability, from the voters to the ultimate policy makers, in which at each stage a principal delegates to an agent. A shortcoming of this linkage, implicitly recognised by Strom, is that it applies to parliamentary democracies.

5 There are different definitions of oversight in the literature (see Olson, 2008) and different meanings in different legislative systems. Nevertheless, Ogul (1976: 11) usefully defined legislative oversight as "the behavior of legislators and their staffs, individually or collectively, which results in an impact, intended or not, on bureaucratic behavior, which affects executive behavior". Legislative oversight thus includes the legislature's review and evaluation of selected activities of the government, both before and during the policy-making phase and the subsequent policy implementation phase. Its goal is to ensure that the government and its agencies, as agents, remain responsive and accountable to citizens directly and to the legislature, as principals (Ogul and Rockman, 1990).

6 However, as Mulgan (1997) stresses, people of equal status may be accountable to one another as part of a mutual authority relationship as long as each accepts the authority of the other.

7 Meier and Hill (2005) go further in their criticism of the principal-agent model. These authors recognise that the basic idea behind the model is that all relationships can be reduced to contractual terms and, therefore, that bureaucracy does not matter. They note that the model "... miss[es] the informal side of bureaucracy, the relationships among individuals that are based on affect and trust" (2005: 60) and point out three additional problems regarding the principal-agent theory. First, the notions of information asymmetry and goal conflict within the model inevitably lead to shirking and negligence on behalf of the agent. But, "in many cases, the real problem is the agent will act even more than the principal seeks" (p. 60). Second, the model misses the element of coercion in bureaucracies: "[t]he model was designed to examine voluntary relationships between equals in a market-like setting. In this case it is applied to mandatory relationships between unequals in a non-market-like situation" (p. 60). Finally, agents often provide what principals want, not for contractual reasons but "... for normative reasons or because the principal's demands are within the agents' zone of acceptance" (p. 60).

3 Legislative oversight tools

1 There are other frameworks for analysing oversight besides those based on "internal" and "external" factors. For example, McCubbins and Schwartz's (1984) propose a distinction between "Police Patrols" and "Fire Alarms" models of oversight. Police Patrols oversight is defined as centralised, active and direct. For instance, a legislature examines a sample of executive agency activities with the aim of detecting and remedying any violations of legislative goals and, by its surveillance, discouraging such violations. On the other hand, the Fire Alarms model is less centralised, and involves less active and direct intervention. In this model, the legislature establishes a system of rules, procedures and informal practices that enables individual citizens and organised interest groups to examine administrative decisions, charge for violations, and seek remedies from agencies, courts and the legislature itself. The legislature then waits for someone to pull the "alarm", indicating that there is a problem requiring investigation (e.g. through a public hearing). This may lead observers to (perhaps mistakenly) view the legislature as not sufficiently

exercising its oversight role. Yet proponents of this view argue that legislatures are more likely to get involved in oversight when it is worthwhile to them, in terms of gaining political support from such activities. The Fire Alarms model increases the likelihood that oversight time is spent on issues important to constituents, and that legislators will get "credit for redressing grievances". However, these two models are not mutually exclusive and most legislatures use a combination of the two.

2 We use the terms ombuds office, ombuds and ombudsperson interchangeably.

3 Comment made to the authors by Navin Beekarry, former director of the anti-corruption agency in Mauritius.

4 Other names for the ombudsperson include Defensor del Pueblo in several Spanish-speaking countries (e.g. Spain, Argentina, Peru and Colombia), Parliamentary Commissioner for Administration (Sri Lanka, United Kingdom), Médiateur de la République (e.g. France, Gabon, Mauritania, Senegal), Public Protector (South Africa), Protecteur du Citoyen (Québec), Volksanwaltschaft (Austria), Public Complaints Commission (Nigeria), Provedor de Justiça (Portugal), Difensore Civico (Italy), Investigator-General (Zambia), Citizen's Aide (Iowa), Wafaqi Mohtasib (Pakistan) and Lok Ayukta (India).

5 For example, this is the case in Belgium, France, Germany, Hungary, Ireland, Italy, Japan, Luxembourg, the Netherlands, Portugal and Switzerland.

6 Don Wolfensberger, director of the Congress Project at the Woodrow Wilson International Center for Scholars and former staff director of the House Rules Committee, explains that the US Congress has not yet adopted a question period for government ministers. Proposals calling for a question period for members of the Cabinet were introduced by Rep. Estes Kefauver (D-Tenn.) in the 1940s, Sen. Walter Mondale (D-Minn.) in the mid-1970s and, most recently, by Rep. Sam Gejdenson (D-Conn.) in 1991 (with then-Rep. Schumer as one of 40 co-sponsors). The House Rules Committee conducted a full-fledged hearing on this last proposal. However, members seemed satisfied that the Congressional committee system is the best mechanism for eliciting information from Cabinet members (see the bimonthly column on procedural politics from Roll Call, "*How Much Did the Yanks Really Split From the Brits in 1776?*", 2 July, 2007).

7 Some scholars, such as Doering (1995) and Wang (2005), include agenda setting as an important factor affecting legislative oversight. However, since this is not an oversight tool but a procedural mechanism, and because of the difficulty in operationalising this variable internationally, I do not include it here.

8 As during question time, "the Speaker (President) of the Parliament plays a key role in … ensure[ing] the smooth progression of parliamentary debates and is vested with wide powers and authority to this end (e.g., right to invite or curtail speeches by members)" (OECD, 2001).

9 The 2001 survey sought information only on seven oversight tools and complete information was collected only for 49 of the 83 legislatures that participated in the survey.

10 Our findings are highly consistent with what was reported by Pelizzo and Stapenhurst (2008). In that study it was reported that questions were employed in 96 per cent of legislatures – a value quite similar to the 96.7 per cent that we found by analysis of the 2009 survey data. Similarly, our estimates as to how common interpellations and ombudsmen really are fairly

similar to the values reported in previous studies (Pelizzo and Stapenhurst, 2008:14) indicated that interpellations and ombudsmen were to be found respectively in 75 and 73 per cent of the legislatures surveyed in 2001. These values are fairly close to data presented in table 3.2.

11 The data that we have used to compute these averages are the responses provided by the respondents, that is, by the clerks of the various legislatures that were surveyed in the course of this research. A cursory look at the data presented in table 3.4 makes it clear such responses were somewhat puzzling.

4 Legislative oversight and the quality of democracy

1 An excellent discussion of this literature, its main points and its limits, can be found in Burnell (2009).

2 The literature concerning what are alternatively called transitions to democracy or democratic transitions, a literature that became associated with the term transitology, has attempted to explain democratic transitions on the ground of macro, or structural, conditions, as well as on the basis of micro conditions. Macro-level explanations of democratic transitions basically posit that the single most important, if not the only, determinant of a democratic transition is represented by the existing set of structural conditions. The most important argument in this regard was presented by Lipset (1959) who suggested that socio-economic development transforms society, makes it more pluralistic, more literate, makes society develop pro-democratic values and creates a demand for democracy. In the words of O'Donnell, development creates the conditions for the pluralisation of society which, in its turn, creates the condition for "the activation of more political actors" (O'Donnell, 1973: 71) as "political pluralization is the political expression of social differentiation" (O'Donnell, 1973: 72). This newly developed demand for democracy eventually leads to the breakdown of the non-democratic regime and to a transition to another regime (Huntington, 1991). When this transition ends with the establishment of a democratic regime, the transition is said to be democratic. While this line of thinking, which was popularised by modernisation theorists, holds that the breakdown of non-democratic regimes is a consequence of their ability to promote socio-economic development, transitologists have also noted that transition to democracy can also be triggered by economic crises (Huntington, 1991). Important as they have been, macro-level explanations have been criticised for being overly deterministic and for neglecting agency. Micro-level explanations have hence suggested that while macro-level factors can create the conditions for having a transition, the relationship between structural conditions and the occurrence of a democratic transition is by no means deterministic. As Morlino (1986) explained, structural conditions can create an opportunity for a democratic transition to occur, but whether the transition in the end takes place or not, whether it leads to the estblishment of a democratic regime or not, depends entirely on the strategic interaction between various sets of actors. Przeworski (1991) famously noted that it is the interaction of hardliners, softliners and civil society that determines whether a transition ultimately occurs or not.

3 While the literature has emphasised that democracy is more likely to become consolidated and survive in countries that are more affluent (Lipset, 1959;

Przeworski *et al.*, 2000), the literature has also made clear that socio-economic conditions are not the only determinant of democratic consolidation and survival. For example, some scholars have noted that whether a newly established democracy is able to consolidate and survive or not depends entirely on how the transition to democracy occurred. Przeworski (1991), for example, noted in this regard that transitions, the periods between the collapse of a regime and the establishment of a new one are "strategic situations that arise when a dictatorship collapses" and that stable democracy is only one of the possible outcomes. Transitions may in fact allow the authoritarian regime to stay in power, they may be conducive to the establishment of a new dictatorship, they may lead to a non self-sustaining democracy (which will eventually fall) or it may end with a stable democracy. According to Przeworski, the establishment of a self-sustaining, and hence stable, democracy occurs only when the reformers in the authoritarian camp ally with the moderates in the democratic camp, because that is the only instance in which democracy with guarantees is established.

4 See our discussion in Chapter 1.

5 The framework hence acknowledges that democratic regimes may differ from one another not only on the basis of the presence/absence of various democratic qualities, but also on the basis of the extent to which these qualities are present/absent.

6 Lijphart (1999) suggested that the Gastil index can be used to assess the quality of democracy, though it is not a terribly useful tool if one wishes to detect some variation in the family of liberal democratic regimes.

7 The regression model takes the following values: 4.225 + .200 number of tools. The significance level of the number of tools variable is .169.

5 Legislative oversight and corruption

1 In his seminal work on modernization, Huntington made the well-known claim, "In terms of economic growth, the only thing worse than a society with a rigid, overcentralized, dishonest bureaucracy is one with a rigid, overcentralized, honest bureaucracy. A society which is relatively uncorrupt … may find a certain amount of corruption a welcome lubricant easing the path to modernization."

2 During many transitions from communism, for example, budget shortfalls meant that public sector works were not paid for months at a time, which made bureaucrats more vulnerable to corruption. See World Bank, 2000: 29.

3 A similar line of thinking was developed by Samuel Huntington (1991), who argued that in very poor countries citizens are so concerned with basic needs that they do not really care about whether the government is democratic or not.

6 Legislative oversight in Ghana

1 This calculation is made from the last military regime (1981–92). Overall, the periods of military government have been 1966–69, 1972–79 and 1981–92. The periods of democratic rule are 1969–72, 1979–81 and 1992–present.

2 Freedom House defines freedom as "the opportunity to act spontaneously in a variety of fields outside the control of government and other centers of

potential domination" in accordance with individuals' political rights and civil liberties. The ratings process is based on 10 questions on political rights and 15 questions on civil liberties. Under political rights, three questions relate to the electoral process, four to political pluralism and three to functioning government. The questions on civil liberties are distributed as follows: four on freedom of expression and beliefs, three on associational and organisations' rights, and four on rule of law. Raw points (0 to 4) are awarded to each. Zero is the smallest and four is the highest on the scale. The highest score attainable under political rights is 40 and 60 under civil liberties. The raw points from the previous years are used as benchmarks for the year under review. Changes to the raw points are only made if major political issues occur in the country under review. The raw data is used to rate countries according to the following scale: 1.0 – 2.5 free; 3.0 – 5.0 partly free; and 5.5 to 7.0 not free. For further details on the methodology, see www.freedomhouse.org.

3 For further details, see Afrobarometer webpage at www.afrobarometer.org.

4 On the 14 standing committees see art. 152 (2) of the Standing Orders, on the 19 select committees see art 153 of the Standing Orders, while the dispositions concerning membership in committees can be found in articles 154 (1) and 154 (2).

5 In 2009, the Inter-Parliamentary Union (IPU) in collaboration with WBI administered a survey questionnaire that was completed by 120 legislatures worldwide. The purpose of this survey was to update and improve the information that IPU and WBI had collected in a survey administered in 2001 and had been used in several WBI publications (Pelizzo and Stapenhurst, 2004; Pelizzo and Stapenhurst, 2008). The 2009 survey on parliamentary oversight consisted of 80 questions, distributed across 10 sections, pertaining respectively to the political system, the government accountability to parliament, the presence/use of motions of censure, the parliament's power of dismissal, the dispositions concerning the parliament's dissolution, tools for parliamentary oversight, the presence of additional oversight bodies, the tools of budgetary oversight, the existence/implementation of a legislative code of conduct and oversight on the implementation of the enacted legislation.

6 Without stable majorities in parliament, the executive is required to bargain with the minority and forge mutually beneficial compromises. By implication, the executive will have to make concessions – and the minority is able to extract compromises that are otherwise inadmissible. Undoubtedly, this strengthens the oversight process (Wehner, 2005) although it carries the risk of gridlock. Bargaining creates opportunities for oversight and enables the minority to hold the government accountable (NDI, 2000).

7 The regulations concerning parliamentary questions can be found in articles 60–69 of the Standing Orders, the dispositions concerning motions for debate can be found in articles 49–50, while articles 152–96 regulate the functioning of parliamentary committees.

8 A deadline of 30 days is set for Benin, Burkina Faso, Côte d'Ivoire, Gabon, Senegal and Togo; for Burundi the deadline is between 28 and 46 days; it is of 14 days for Uganda, of 15 days for Cameroon, of 10 days for Kenya and 7 days for Namibia. The respondent for Congo claimed that the deadline for answering a written question in Congo is of 1 day only.

9 The importance of the power to review presidential nominations and appointment was emphasised in the course of personal communications to

one of the authors as well as in response to question 47 of the IPU-WBI survey conducted in 2009.

10 As the respondent noted in responding to question 62 of the IPU-WBI survey.

11 The relationship between oversight potential, the amount of oversight activities performed and the effectiveness of oversight has been subject to some disagreement. While it is clear that legislative oversight cannot be effective if it is never performed, and that it cannot be performed if a legislature does not have adequate oversight tools, it is much less clear whether and how oversight potential, activity and effectiveness are actually related to one another. Sartori (1987), for example, suggested that what is important, with regard to legislative oversight, is not how frequently it is performed but whether a parliament has oversight potential that can be used if necessary. Sartori in fact believed that if a legislature spent too much time performing its oversight activities, it would dissipate its energy and resources and undermine the effectiveness of its actions. Some evidence on the inverse relationship between amount of oversight activity performed and its effectiveness can be found in Pelizzo (2008). If instead of focusing on legislative oversight out of court, one were to focus exclusively on the oversight of public expenditures and public accounts committees, the relationship between potential, activity and effectiveness has been addressed in Pelizzo (2010a) for the PACs of the Pacific Island states and in Pelizzo (2011) for the PACs of the Commonwealth.

12 The data collected by WBI on PACs and that were used in Pelizzo (2011) show that in the three years from 1999–2002, the PAC met more than 50 times, that is more frequently than Botswana and Namibia and as frequently as the PACs from Kenya, Mozambique, Nigeria and South Africa. The data presented in that paper also suggest that the PAC from Ghana is considerably more effective than its Namibian and Nigerian counterparts. A new survey conducted in 2009 collected information on PACs' activity and effectiveness for the 2006–8 period, but the data have not yet been made available for analysis.

13 McGee (2002) had long suggested, and subsequent studies repeated, that opening PAC meetings to the media is crucial in securing PACs' successful performance.

14 Interestingly, the public disgust at the government prompted by the PAC's public hearing led the government to order the termination of live broadcasts on the state-run television channel. Unfortunately, the proliferation of private TV and radio stations in the country permitted continuous live broadcasts of the hearings. The government reversed its order to terminate live broadcasts on the state-run TV channel and sought to associate itself with the decision to hold public hearings as further proof of its zero-tolerance policy on corruption.

15 For further details, see The Statesman newspaper dated 17 October 2007. This news report is also available online at www.ghanaweb.com.

16 For details of the report, see Ghana News Agency report entitled "PAC Recovers 40m from public servants", 5 November 2008, available online at www.ghanaweb.com.

17 This seemingly strange score – that parliament amends the budget fairly frequently, suggests that many respondents do not realise that amendments are rare.

18 This seemingly strange score – that parliament over-rides presidential vetoes frequently, suggests that many respondents do not realise that such over-rides are rare.

19 The Afrobarometer surveys have been conducted in Ghana in 1999, 2002, 2005 and 2008.

20 Under its Standing Orders, parliament has the authority to establish special or ad hoc committees to "investigate any matter of public importance, to consider any Bill that does not come under the jurisdiction of any of the standing or select committees" (Standing Order 191). The most famous example of a special committee in parliament is the Committee on Poverty Alleviation. (The committee is now a standing committee in parliament.)

21 The Parliamentary Centre is noted for its immense contribution, in collaboration with other international donor agencies, to improving the capacity of MPs to perform their assignments through a combination of seminars, workshops and international exposure.

22 Namely, impact on legislation, budget amendment and appointment of ministers and senior judges.

23 The first two Speakers of Parliament after 1992 were Rt. Hon Justice D.F. Annan and Rt. Hon. Pete Ala Djetey, both of whom were successful in increasing parliament's powers vis-à-vis the executive. The third Speaker, Ebenezer Hughes, by contrast "played it safe along the wishes of the Executive" (Lindberg and Zhou, 2009).

24 This PAC's activism lead to greater public awareness regarding the role of parliament in contemporary governance, including its potential and limitations.

25 Effective oversight may depend on the specific oversight powers given to the parliament, on whether the parliament has the ability to modify legislation (Loewenberg and Patterson, 1979), on whether parliaments and parliamentarians are given proper information to perform their oversight tasks adequately (Frantzich, 1979), on the role of individual MPs, on the role of committee chairs, on the saliency of issues and on how aggressively the opposition performs its role (Rockman, 1984).

7 A strategic interaction model

1 Harry Eckstein, one of the most important proponents of the culturalist approach, recognised that political culture theory has often coped inadequately with change. In this respect, he quoted Rogowski's idea that "culturalists have been very offhand in dealing with change – [that] they have tended to improvise far too much in order to accommodate political changes into their framework. They have done so, he writes, to the point that they no longer have a convincing way to treat political change at all." Eckstein went on to say that "this argument – and others to similar effect – strikes me as cogent criticism of how culturalists have in fact dealt with political changes. Furthermore, difficulties accounting for change in general and for certain kinds of change especially seem to me inherent in the assumptions on which the political culture approach is based" (Eckstein, 1988: 789–90).

2 On this point see, Boettke, Coyne and Leeson (2008).

3 The idea that an institutional setting and/or a constitutional order is self-sustaining only if it emerges from the context in which it has to operate was

initially proposed by Hayek (1978). Hayek in fact suggested that the only necessary condition for a self-sustaining political, institutional and constitutional order is that order was self-generating or spontaneous.

8 Testing the model – Public Accounts Committees

1 For a definition of legitimacy, see Lipset (1959). On the importance of legitimacy for the consolidation and the survival of political regimes, both democratic and otherwise, see Lipset (1959) and Huntington (1991). For a discussion of the various sources of legitimacy, see Huntington (1991) which also provides an insightful discussion of the factors that may erode the legitimacy of a political regime.

2 The 1993 electoral reform in Italy or the abolition of state subsidies to party organizations in Italy in 1993 were both, in many respects, the consequence of the legitimacy crisis that had emerged in the course of the Bribesville scandal and that led eventually to the disappearance and/or the transformation of all Italian traditional parties. What matters for our present purposes is, however, the fact that a political class that long resisted the pressure to reform itself and introduce a comprehensive set of institutional reforms in the wake of the crisis and the loss of legitimacy no longer had the strength and the power to preserve the status quo.

3 In his work, Hardman (1986: 155) observed that "the envisaged institutional reforms (such as parliamentary control of finance, establishment of the office of Auditor-General and formation of Public Accounts Committee) eventuated and are still in force. However sedulous adherence to conventional Westminster forms and mechanisms in financial legislation on and after self-government … precluded the emergence of innovatory measures specifically addressing indigenous development and cultural preservation." Hardman (1986) went on to argue that the financial legislation modelled after that of the former colonial powers was inadequate, that financial control was inefficient, and that more effective financial scrutiny could be provided by developing local solutions to local conditions.

4 The evidence generated in Degeling, Anderson and Guthrie (1996) did indeed show that the activities performed by PAC varied over time, but the judgment of whether one PAC was more effective than another was, to a large extent, a function of the categorisation proposed by the authors. The authors' *a priori* judgment of what is effective financial scrutiny would have been much more convincing if they had made an effort to cross-validate, on some objective ground, their expert opinion. Even assuming that their taxonomic effort was correct, and that certain types of financial scrutiny have indeed more bite than others, the authors did not perform any quantitative analysis to identify the determinants of effective financial scrutiny.

5 A conclusion that, we believe, is perfectly consistent with what Hardmann (1984a, 1984b and 1986) was arguing.

6 The study conducted by Pelizzo *et al.* (2006: 781) showed that PACs' recommendations were accepted frequently in 78.8% of the cases, that PACs' recommendations were implemented in 63.6% of the cases, that better information was provided to the PAC in the wake of its reports in 60.8% of the cases, that disciplinary action was taken in 27.3% of the cases and that PACs' activity led to the modification of legislation in 15.3% of the cases.

7 Devised by Global Integrity.

8 The study of PACs in Pacific Island States highlighted that some indicators of activity were negatively, albeit insignificantly, related to the range of formal powers available to the PACs. Had this evidence been statistically significant, it would have sustained the claim that precisely where PACs are stronger, have a wider range of powers, they are less likely to use them. Hence the task facing the international community and practitioners is not so much that of strengthening legislatures by expanding their oversight capacity, but is that of ensuring that legislatures and legislative committees make effective use of whatever powers they may have.

9 The two organizations sent a survey questionnaire to national and sub-national legislatures in Commonwealth countries from Africa, Asia, Australasia, the British Isles and Canada.

10 Fifty-four responses were received, 24 of which were provided by national legislatures. The survey included 61 questions grouped under 12 different headings and were meant to provide information in a variety of respects, such as the composition of the committee, the powers assigned to the committee, the practices of the committee and the frequency with which the committee was able to achieve certain results. Respondents were also asked to provide some information as to how important certain conditions were for the achievement of those results. About two-thirds of the legislatures included in the survey provided usable information.

11 Hence the importance of an opposition Chair becomes a proxy for the level of good governance in a country.

12 Hence, the reform of the office of the AG in Finland, the reform of the Finnish version of a PAC, the discussion in the Italian parliament of a project of law designed to introduce greater legislative scrutiny of public spending and to ensure greater transparency in the public accounts, the adoption of a PAC in Indonesia, are all just examples that sustain the theoretical claims advanced by our model.

13 It is true, of course, that in Vanuatu the PAC was not convened in the 2000–3 period and that, when it resumed operations, it had to audit the accounts of the 1994–7 period, but it is also true that before it interrupted its operations, the PAC of Vanuatu was auditing the accounts of the 1986–94 period. In other words, the PAC were not timely either before or after their operations were interrupted.

14 Information concerning these cases was gathered from the online version of the *Solomon Star News* from 14 and 15 October 2008. See Moffat Mamu, "Where's $200,000?", *Solomon Star*, 14 October 2008; "Audit raises questions over use of public assets", *Solomon Star*, 14 October 2008; "Where's the $189,000 imprest?", *Solomon Star*, 15 October 2008. There were also some unsigned articles that reported the daily activities of the Auditor General: "More MPs help themselves with forestry money", *Solomon Star*, 15 October 2008; "Ghiro: Blame Ministry of Finance", *Solomon Star*, 15 October 2008.

9 Conclusions

1 The literature on PAC, and above all McGee (2002), made clear that one of the reasons why MPs do not want to serve on a PAC is that they fear that

serving on such a committee may jeopardise their chances to be re-elected. This is an instance of a broader phenomenon, namely that MPs fear that by engaging in anti-corruption activities or by advocating anti-corruption reforms, they may put their lives and careers at risk and therefore are somewhat reluctant to do anything to promote good governance in their country. As we noted earlier on, at the end of one international seminar on good governance once of us approached an MP and asked him whether he needed or wanted materials to promote and advocate good governance back home and the MP politely declined the invitation for he did not have any intention of losing either his life or his parliamentary seat. Obviously, the MP in question had this type of fear because in his country there was no overt popular demand for good governance and he feared that promoting good governance would involve many risks without providing any tangible benefit. Obviously, once a demand for good governance has emerged and members of the ruling elite/political class are able to see that by promoting good governance they can enjoy major benefits and have greater electoral returns, they are confronted with a very different set of incentives and are much more likely to support a departure from the institutional status quo.

2 In this respect, our position is somewhat different from Huntington (1968), Panebianco (1983) and Piattoni (2007). Each of these authors treats political corruption, vote buying and similar forms of unethical/illicit behavior as byproducts of inadequate institutionalisation and political development. The obvious implication in the Huntington-Panebianco-Piattoni line of thinking is that once political organisations are adequately developed and institutionalised, all the problems associated with poor institutionalisation automatically disappear. This idea is fairly similar to what Norbert Elias (2000) said with regard to the process of civilisation and the development of so-called good manners. For Elias, civilisation was a somewhat linear process that occurred incrementally over time, and that consisted in (removing from the public sphere and in the) disappearance of those types of behaviour that were no longer consistent with the sensibility of society. Both accounts, that is, Elias's account of the civilising process and the development of good manners and the Huntington-Panebianco-Piattoni account of poor institutionalisation–corruption nexus, leave no role for agency. Agency is at best a residual category. It is understandable why a sociologist interested in historical dynamics may see little value in agency. It is much less understandable why three brilliant political scientists left little room for agency. This is where our analysis departs from the Huntington-Panebianco-Piattoni line of thinking: we agree with them on the fact that corruption is a consequence of poor institutionalisation and inadequate political development, but we disagree on the role of agency. While they neglect the role of agential factors, we argue instead that under proper conditions agents can play a key role in passing anti-corruption reforms and implementing them effectively – even in societies that are not known for their political development.

Bibliography

Africa Report, The. October 2006.

Afrobaramoter (2009) *Surveys.* www.afrobarometer.org/surveys.html.

Almond, Gabriel, and Sydney Verba (1963) *The Civic Culture.* Princeton: Princeton University Press.

Berle, A., and Gardner Means (1932) *The Modern Corporation and Private Property.* New York, NY: Macmillan.

Blondel, J. (1973) *Comparative Legislatures.* Englewood Cliffs, NJ: Prentice Hall.

Blume, L., and S. Voight (2007) "Supreme Audit Institutions: Supremely Superfluous: A Cross Country Assessment." *ICER Working Papers 2003–07.*

Blyth, M. (2002) *Great Transformations.* New York: Cambridge University Press.

Boettke, P. J., and V. H. Storr (2002) "Post Classical Political Economy." *American Journal of Economics and Sociology* 61.1: 161–91.

Boettke, P. J., C. J. Coyne and P. T. Leeson (2008) "Institutional Stickiness and the New Development Economics." *American Journal of Economics and Sociology* 67.2: 331–58.

Bovens, M. (2005a) "Public Accountability." In E. Ferlie, L. Lynn Jr and C. Pollitt (eds), *The Oxford Handbook of Public Management,* 182–208. Oxford: Oxford University Press.

——(2005b) "Public Accountability:A Framework for the Analysis and Assessment of Accountability Arrangements in the Public Domain." Prepared for CONNEX, Research Group 2: *Democracy and Accountability in the EU.*

——(2006) "Analyzing and Assessing Public Accountability: A Conceptual Framework." *European Governance Papers* (EUROGOV), No. C-06-01.

Bratton, M. (2007) "The Democracy Barometers: Formal versus Informal Institutions in Africa." *Journal of Democracy* 18.3: 98–110.

Burnell, P. (2009) "Legislative Strengthening Meets Party Support in International Assistance." *Journal of Legislative Studies* 15.4: 460–80.

Carothers, T (2009) "Democratic Assistance: Political vs. Developmental." *Journal of Democracy* 20.1: 5–19.

Cavill, S., and M. Sohail (2004) "Strengthening Accountability for Urban Services." *Environment and Urbanization* 16.1: 155–70.

Chabal, P., D. Birmingham, J. Forrest, M. Newitt, G. Seibert and E. Adrade (2002) *A History of Postcolonial Lusophone Africa*. Bloomington, IN: Indiana University Press.

Chabal, P., and J-P. Daloz (1999) *Africa Works*. Oxford: James Currey for the International Africa Institute.Crowther, W., and D. Olson (2002) "Committees in New Democratic Parliaments; Comparative Institutionalization." In D. Olson and W. Crowther (eds), *Committees in Post-Communist Democratic Parliaments: Comparative Institutionalization*, 176–206. Columbus, OH: Ohio State University.

Cutright, P. (1965) "Political Structure, Economic Development and National Security Problems." *American Journal of Sociology* 70.5: 537–50.

D'Aunno, T., R. Sutton and R. Price (1991) "Isomorphism and External Support in Conflicting Institutional Environments: A Study of Drug Abuse Treatment Units." *Academy of Management Journal* 34: 636–61.

Degeling, P., J. Anderson and J. Guthrie (1996) "Accounting for Public Accounts Committees." *Accounting, Auditing and Accountability Journal* 9.2: 30–49.

DiMaggio, P., and W. W. Powell (1983) "The Iron Cage Revisited: Institutional Isomorphism and Collective Rationality in Organizational Fields." *American Sociological Review* 48: 147–60.

——(1991) "Introduction." In W. W. Powell and P. J. DiMaggio (eds.), *The New Institutionalism in Organizational Analysis*, 1–40. Chicago: University of Chicago Press.

Doering, H. (ed.) (1995) *Parliaments and Majority Rule in Western Europe*. New York, NY: St Martins P.Drewry, G. (ed.) (1989) *The New Select Committees*. Oxford: Clarendon Press.

Dubrow, G. (2001) "Systems of Governance and Parliamentary Accountability." In *Parliamentary Accountability and Good Governance: A Parliamentarians Handbook*, 23–30. Washington, DC and Ottawa: World Bank Institute and Parliamentary Centre.

Duverger, M. (1954) *Political Parties*. New York: Wiley.

——(1980) "New Political System Model: Semi-Presidential Government." *European Journal of Political Research* 8.2: 165–87.

Eckstein, Harry (1988) "A Culturalist Theory of Political Change." *American Political Science Review* 82.3: 789–804.

Elias, N. (2000) *The Civilizing Process*. London: Blackwell and Wiley.

Evans, H. (1999) "Parliament and Extra-Parliamentary Accountability Institutions." Paper presented at the Accountability in Australian Government Symposium, National Council of the Institute of Public Administration, Brisbane, Australia.

Finer, Herman, (1932) *The Theory and the Practice of Modern Government*. London: Methuen.

Fish, S. (2006) "Stronger Legislatures, Stronger Democracy." *Journal of Democracy* 17.1: 5–20.

Frantzich, S. E. (1979) "Computerized Information Technology in the U.S. House of Representatives." *Legislative Studies Quarterly* 4.2: 295–330.

Friedman, E., S. Johnson, D. Kaufmann and P. Zoido-Lobaton (2000) "Dodging the Grabbing Hand: the Determinants of Unofficial Activity in 69 Countries." *Journal of Public Economics* 76: 459–93.

Fukuyama, F. (2004a) "Why There Is No Science of Public Administration." *Journal of International Affairs* 58.1: 189–201.

——(2004b) *State-Building, Governance and World Order in the 21st. Century.* Ithaca, NY: Cornell University Press.

Gerring, J., and S. Thacker (2004) "Political Institutions and Corruption: The Role of Unitism and Parliamentarism." *British Journal of Political Science* 34: 295–330.

Gerring, J., S. Thacker and C. Moreno (2005) "A Centripetal Theory of Democratic Governance: A Global Inquiry." *American Political Science Review* (Nov.): 567–81.

Goetz, A. M., and J. Gaventa (2001) "Bringing Citizen Voice and Client Focus into Service Delivery." *IDS Working Paper No. 138.* Brighton: University of Sussex.

Granovetter, M. (1985) "Economic Action and Social Structure: The Problem of Embeddedness." *American Journal of Sociology* 91.3: 481–510.

Gyimah-Boadi, E. (2001) "A Peaceful Turnover in Ghana." *Journal of Democracy* 12.2: 103–17.

Hall, P., and R. Taylor (1996) "Political Science and the Three New Institutionalisms." *Political Studies* 44.5: 936–37.

Hamilton, A., and R. Stapenhurst (2011) "New and Non-commonwealth PACs." Unpublished manuscript.Hardman, D. J. (1984a) "Canberra to Port Moresby: Government Accounting and Budgeting for the Early Stages of Devolution." *Accounting and Finance* 24.2: 75–97.

——(1984b) "Public Financial Administration of Microstates: South Pacific Forum." *Public Administration and Development* 4.1: 141–54.

——(1986) "Paradigms of public financial administration in the evolution of Papua New Guinea." *Public Administration and Development* 6.2: 151–61.

Hayek, F. (1978) *Law, Legislation and Liberty.* Chicago: University of Chicago Press.

Heilbrunn, J. (2004) "Anti-Corruption Agencies." *World Bank Institute Working Paper.*

Hellman, J. S., G. Jones and D. Kaufmann (2000) "Seize the State, Seize the Day – An Empirical Analysis of State Capture and Corruption in Transition." *World Bank Policy Research Working Paper* 2444, September.

Hermens, Ferdinand A. (1941) *Democracy or Anarchy?* South Bend: University of Notre Dame Press.

Hubli, Scott, and Martin Schmidt (2007) "Approaches to Legislative Strengthening, Department for Democracy and Social Development: SIDA Evaluation 05/27.2005."

Huntington, S. P. (1968) *Political Order in Changing Societies.* New Haven, CT: Yale University Press.

——(1991) *The Third Wave of Democratization.* London: University of Oklahoma Press.

Inter-Parliamentary Union (2006) *Parliament and Democracy in the 21st. Century: A Good Practice Guide.* Geneva: IPU.

Jacobs, K., and K. Jones (2009) "Legitimacy and Parliamentary Oversight in Australia: the Rise and Fall of Two Public Accounts Committees." *Accounting, Auditing and Accountability Journal* 22.1: 13–34.

Jacobs, K., K. Jones and X. Smith (2010) " An Analysis of The Sources of Public Accounts Committee Inquiries: The Australian Experience." *Australasian Parliamentary Review* 25.1: 17–31.

Jensen, M., and P. Meckling (1976) "The Theory of the Firm: Managerial Behavior, Agency Costs, and Ownership Structure." *Journal of Financial Economics* 3: 305–60.

Johnson, John K., and Robert Nakamura (2006) *Orientation Handbook for Member of Parliament.* Washington, DC: World Bank Institute.Johnson, S. Kaufmann, D. McMillan and C. Woodruff (2003) "Why Do Firms Hide? Bribes and Unofficial Activity after Communism." *Public Economics EconWPA 0308004.* Washington, DC: World Bank.

Johnston, M. (1993) "What Can be Done About Entrenched Corruption?" *Paper presented at the World Bank.*

Johnston, M., and S. Kpundeh (2001) "Anti-Corruption Coalitions and Reforms." Unpublished manuscript.

Johnston, N., and L. von Trapp (2008) *Strengthening Parliament-Strengthening Accountability.* Washington, DC: World Bank Institute.

Kaufmann, D. (1997) *Corruption: The Facts.* Foreign Policy, 107; Washington, DC: Carnegie Endowment for International Peace.

——(2000) "World Bank Institute Foreword." In R. Klitgaard, R. MacLean-Aboroa and L. Parris (eds), *Corrupt Cities: A Practical Guide to Cure and Prevention*, viii–x. Oakland, CA: Institute for Contemporary Studies Press.

——(2006) "Myths and Realities of Governance and Corruption" In *The World Economic Forum Global Competitiveness Report 2005–6.* New York: World Economic Forum.

Knill, Christopher, and Andrea Lenschow (2001) "Seek and Ye Shall Find! Linking Different Perspectives on Institutional Change." *Comparative Political Studies* 34.2: 187–215.

KPMG (2006) "The Parliamentary Public Accounts Committee; An Australian and New Zealand Perspective." KPMG Australia.

Krafchik, W. (2003) "What Role Can Civil Society and Parliament Play in Strengthening the External Audit Function?" Paper presented at African regional workshop, *Towards Auditing Effectiveness*, organised by the World Bank Institute and held in Ethiopia 12–15 May 2003. Washington, DC: International Budget Project.

Kuczynski, P. P., and J. Williamson (2003) "After the Washington Consensus. Restarting Growth and Reform in Latin America." *Institute for International Economics.* Washington, DC.

Kuhn, T. (1962) *The Structure of Scientific Revolution.* Chicago: University of Chicago Press.

Kunicova, J., and S. Rose-Ackerman (2005) "Electoral Rules and Constitutional Structures as Constraints on Corruption." *British Journal of Political Science* 35: 573–606.

LaPalombara, J. (1974) *Politics within Nations.* Englewood Cliffs, NJ: Prentice Hall.

Lederman, D., N. Loayza and Soares, R. (2001) "Accountability and Corruption: Political Institutions Do Matter." *Policy Research Working Paper 2708.* Washington, DC: World Bank.

——(2005) "Accountability and Corruption: Political Institutions Do Matter." *Economics and Politics* 17: 1–35l.

Lijphart, A. (1999) *Patterns of Democarcy.* New Haven: Yale University Press.

Lindberg, S. I., and Y. Zhou (2009) "Co-optation Despite Democrtization in Ghana." In J. Barkan (ed.), *Legislatures in Emerging Democracies,* 147–75. Boulder, CO: Lynne Rienner.

Linz, Juan J. (1994) "Presidential or Parliamentary Democracy: Does it Make a Difference?" In Juan J. Linz and Arturo Valenzuela (eds), *The Failure of Presidential Democracy,* 1–91. Baltimore: Johns Hopkins University Press.

Lipset, Seymour Martin (1959) "Some Social Requisites of Democracy." *American Political Science Review* 53.1: 69–105.

——(1960) *Political Man: The Social Bases of Politics.* New York: Doubleday.

Lipset, Martin Seymour, and Stein Rokkan (eds) (1967) *Party Systems and Voters Alignment.* New York: Doubleday.

Loewenberg, G., and S. Patterson (1979) *Comparing Legislatures.* Boston, MA: Little Brown.

Lowell, L. (1897) *Governments and Parties in Continental Europe.* Boston: Houghton, Mifflin and Co.

Macridis, Roy C. (1968), "Comparative Politics and the Study of Government: the Search for Focus." *Comparative Politics* 1 (October): 86.

Maffio, R. (2002) "Quis Custodiet ipsos Custodes? Il Controllo Parlamentare dell' Attiva di Governo in Prospettiva Comparata." *Quaderni di Scienza Politica* 9.2: 333–83.

Mahoney, J., and R. Snyder (1999) "Rethinking Agency and Structure in the Study of Regime Change." *Studies in Comparative International Development* 34.2: 3–32.

Mainwaring, Scott (1993) "Presidentialism, Multipartism and Democracy. The Difficult Combination." *Comparative Political Studies* 26.2: 198–228.

Mamu, M. (2008a) "Where's $200,000?" *Solomon Star,* 14 October.

——(2008b) "Audit raises questions over use of public assets." *Solomon Star,* 14 October.

——(2008c) "Where's the $ 189,000 imprest?" *Solomon Star,* 15 October.

March, James, and Johan Olsen (2006) "Elaborating the 'New Institutionalism'." In R. A. W. Rhodes, Sarah Binder and Bert Rockman (eds), *The Oxford Handbook of Political Institutions,* 3–22. Oxford: Oxford University Press.

Matiangi, F. (2006) "Case Study: The Role of Parliament in the Fight against Corruption: The Case of the Kenyan Parliament." In R. Stapenhurst,

N. Johnston and R. Pelizzo (eds), *The Role of Parliament in Curbing Corruption*, 69–77. Washington, DC: World Bank Institute.Mauro, P. (1997) "The Effects of Corruption on Growth, Investment and Government Expenditure: A Cross Country Analysis." In K. A. Ellio (ed.), *Corruption and the Global Economy*, 83–107. Washington, DC: Institute for International Economics.

Mazur, J., and B. Vella (2001) "Relations between SAIs and Parliamentary Committees." In *Report Prepared by SAIs of the Central and Eastern European Countries, Cyprus, Malta and the European Court of Auditors*. Limassol: SIGMA.

——(2003) "Relations between SAIs and Parliamentary Committees." *International Journal of Government Auditing* 30: 16.

McCubbins, M., and T. Schwartz (1984) "Congressional Oversight Overlooked: Police Controls vs. Fire Alarms." *American Journal of Political Science* 28.2: 165–79.

McGee, D. (2002) *The Overseers. Public Account Committees and Public Spending*. London: Pluto Press.

McInnes, S. (1977) "Improving Legislative Surveillance of Provincial Expenditures: The Performance of Public Accounts Committees and Auditors General." *Canadian Public Administration* 20.1: 36–86.

Meagher, P. (2004) "Anti-Corruption Agencies: A Review of Experience." *The IRIS Discussion Papers on Institutions and Development* N. College Park, MD: University of Maryland.

Meier, K. J., and G. C. Hill (2005) "Bureaucracy in the 21st. Century." In E. Ferlie, L. Lynn Jr and C. Pollitt (eds), *The Oxford Handbook of Public Management*. Oxford: Oxford University Press.

Meyer, J., and B. Rowan (1977) "Institutionalized Organizations: Formal Structure as Myth and Ceremony." *American Journal of Sociology* 83: 340–63.

Meyer, J., W. R. Scott and T. Deal (1983) "Institutional and Technical Sources of Organizational Structure." In J. Meyer and W. Scott (eds), *Organization Environment: Ritual and Reality*, 45–70. Philadelphia, PA: Temple University Press.

Moe, T. (1984) "The New Economics of Organization." *American Journal of Political Science* 28: 739–77.

Morlino, Leonardo (1986) "Democrazie." In G. Pasquino (ed.), *Manuale di scienza politica*, 83–136. Bologna: il mulino.

——(2001) "Consolidamento democratico: la teoria dell'ancoraggio." *Quaderni di Scienza Politica* 8.2: 217–47.

——(2005) "Spiegare la qualita' democratica: quanto sono rilevanti le tradizioni autoritarie?" *Rivista Italiana di Scienza Politica* 35.2: 191–212.

——(2010) *Democratization and the European Union*. London and New York: Routledge.

Mulgan, R. (1997) "Processes of Accountability." *Australian Journal of Public Administration* 56.1: 25–36.

——(2003). *Holding Power to Account – Accountability in Modern Democracies*. New York: Palgrave Macmillan.

Murphy, K. M., A. Shleifer and R. W. Vishny (1991) "The Allocation of Talent: Implications for Growth." *The Quarterly Journal of Economics* 106: 503–30.

Naím, M. (1994) "The World Bank: Its Role, Governance and Organizational Culture." *Carnegie Endowment for International Peace.* Washington, DC.

National Democratic Institute (2000) "Strengthening Legislative Capacity in Legislative-Executive Relation." *Legislative Research Series,* paper no. 6. Washington, DC.

Neff, N. H. (1964) "Economic Development through Bureaucratic Corruption." *The American Behavioral Scientist* 8.2: 8–14.

North, D. (1990) *Institutions, Institutional Change and Economic Performance.* New York, NY: Cambridge University Press.

Norton, P. (1998) "Introduction: The Institution of Parliaments." In P. Norton (ed.), *Parliaments and Governments in Western Europe vol. 1,* 1–43. London: Frank Cass.

Norton, P., and N. Ahmed (1999) "Legislatures in Asia: Exploring Diversity." In P. Norton and N. Ahmed (eds), *Legislatures in Developmental Perspective,* 1–12. London: Frank Cass.

O'Brien, Mitchell, Rick Stapenhurst and Niall Johnston (2008), *Parliaments as Peacebuilders in Conflict-Affected Countries.* Washington, DC: World Bank.

O'Donnell, Guillermo (1973) *Modernization and Bureaucratic-Authoritarianism.* Berkeley: Berkeley University Press.

——(1998) "Horizontal Accountability in New Democracies." *Journal of Democracy* 9.3: 112–26.

——(1999) "Horizontal Accountability in New Democracies." In A. Schedler, L. Diamond and M. Plattner (eds), *The Self-Restraining State: Power and Accountability in New Democracies,* 29–52. Boulder, CO: Lynne Rienner.

O'Donnell, Guillermo, and Philippe Schmitter (eds) (1986) *Transitions from Authoritarian Rule. Vol. IV.* Baltimore: Johns Hopkins University Press.

OECD (2001) "Report on Parliamentary Procedures and Relations." *PUMA/LEG (2000)2/REV1.*

Ogul, M. S. (1976) *Congress Oversees the Bureaucracy: Studies in Legislative Supervision.* Pittsburg, PA: University of Pittsburgh Press.

Ogul, M. S., and B. A. Rockman (1990) "Overseeing Oversight: New Departures and Old Problems." *Legislative Studies Quarterly* 15: 5–24.

Olson, D. (2004) "Administrative Review and Oversight: The Experiences of Post-Communist Legislatures." In R. Pelizzo, R. Stapenhurst and D. Olson (eds), *The Role of Parliaments in the Budget Process,* 323–31. World Bank Institute Working Paper; Washington, DC: World Bank.

——(2008) "Legislatures and Administration in Oversight and Budgets: Constraints, Means and Executives." In R. Stapenhurst, R. Pelizzo, D. Olson and L. von Trapp (eds), *Legislative Oversight and Budgeting: A World Perspective,* 323–31. Washington, DC: World Bank.

Olson, D., and P. Norton (eds) (1996) *The New Parliaments of Central and Eastern Europe.* London: Frank Cass.

Olson, D., and M. Mezey (1991) *Legislatures in the Policy Process: Dilemmas of Economic Policy.* Cambridge: Cambridge University Press.

Pacific Islands Forum Secretariat (2010) *PIFS Good Leadership Report: Kiribati*. 24 October. http://www.forumsec.org.fj/resources/uploads/attachments/documents/PIFS_Good_Leadership_Report_Kiribati.pdf.Panebianco, Angelo (1983) *Modelli di partito*. Bologna: il mulino.

Patzelt, W. J. (1994) "A Framework for Comparative Parliamentary Research in Eastern and Central Europe." In A. Agh (ed.), *The Emergence of East Central European Parliaments: The First Steps*, 108–21. Budapest: Hungarian Center of Democracy Studies Foundation.

Pelizzo, R. (2006) "Political Parties." In R. Stapenhurst, N. Johnston and R. Pelizzo (eds), *The Role of Parliament in Curbing Corruption*, 175–84. Washington, DC: World Bank Institute.

——(2008) "Oversight and Democracy Reconsidered." In R. Stapenhurst, R. Pelizzo, D. Olson and L. von Trapp (eds), *Legislative Oversight and Budgeting: A World Perspective*, 29–48. Washington, DC: World Bank.

——(2010a) "Public Accounts Committees in Asia." Paper presented at the Annual Meeting of the Southern Political Science Association, Atlanta, GA.

——(2010b). "Public Accounts Committees in the Pacific Region." *Politics and Policy* 38.1: 117–37.

Pelizzo, R., and Salvatore J. Babones (2007) "The Political Economy of Polarized Pluralism." *Party Politics* 13.1: 53–67.

Pelizzo, R., and R. Stapenhurst (2004) "Legislatures and Oversight: A Note." *Quaderni di Scienza Politica* 11.1: 175–88.

——(2006) "Democracy and Oversight." Paper presented at the annual meeting of the American Political Science Association, Marriott, Loews Philadelphia, and the Pennsylvania Convention Center, Philadelphia, PA, 31 Aug., 2006.

——(2007) "Strengthening Public Accounts Committees by Targetting Regional and Country Specific Weaknesses." In A. Shah (ed.), *Performance Accountability and Combating Corruption*, 379–93. Washington, DC: World Bank.

——(2008) "Tools for Legislative Oversight." In R. Stapenhurst, R. Pelizzo, D. Olson and L. von Trapp (eds), *Legislative Oversight and Budgeting: A World Perspective*, 9–22. Washington, DC: World Bank.

——(2011) "The Activity of Public Accounts Committees in the Commonwealth: Causes and Consequences." *Commonwealth and Comparative Politics* 49.3.

Pelizzo, R., F. Stapenhurst, V. Sahgal and W. Woodley (2006) "What Makes Public Account Committees Work? A Comparative Analysis." *Politics and Policy* 34.4: 774–93.

Piattoni, S. 2007. *Le virtu del clientelismo*. Bari: Laterza.

Przeworski, Adam (1991) *Democracy and the Market*. New York: Cambridge University Press.

Przeworski, Adam, and Fernando Limongi (1993) "Political Regimes and Economic Growth." *Journal of Economic Perspectives* 7.3 (Summer): 51–69.

——(1997) "Modernization. Theories and Facts." *World Politics* 49.2 (January): 155–83.

Przeworski, Adam, Fernando Limongi, Michael Alvarez and Jose' Antonio Cheibub (2000) *Democracy and Development*. New York: Cambridge

University Press.Putnam, R. (1993) *Making Democracy Work: Civic Traditions in Modern Italy*. Princeton, NJ: Princeton University Press.

Rawlings, G. (2006) "Regulating Responsively for Oversight Agencies in the Pacific." Targeted research paper for AusAid, 2006.

Reilly, Benjamin (2006) *Democracy and Diversity: Political Engineering in the Asia-Pacific*. Oxford: Oxford University Press.

Rhodes, R. A., S. A. Binder and B. A. Rockman (2006) *The Oxford Handbook of Political Institutions*. Oxford: Oxford University Press.

Rockman, B. (1984) "Legislative-Executive Relations and Legislative Oversight." *Journal of Legislative Studies* 9.3: 387–440.

Rose-Ackerman, S. (1978) *Corruption. A Study in Political Economy*. London and New York: Academic Press.

——(1999) *Corruption and Government: Causes, Consequences and Reforms*. Cambridge: Cambridge University Press.

Rueschemeyer, D., E. Stephens and J. Stephens (1992) *Capitalist Development and Democracy*. Chicago: University of Chicago Press.

Rustow, D. A. (1968) "Modernization and Comparative Politics: Prospects in Research and Theory." *Comparative Politics* 1.1: 37–52.

Samsudin, R. S., and N. Mohamed (2009) "The Magnitude of Public Account Committee's Work in Reviewing and Reporting on State Governments' Financial Statements." *Malaysian Accounting Review* 8.2: 1–15.

Sanders, E. B. (2006) "Design Research in 2006." *Design Research Quarterly* 1.1: 1–8.

Sartori, G. (1970) "Concept Misinformation in Comparative Politics." *American Political Science Review* 64: 1033–53.

——(1976). *Parties and Party Systems*. New York: Cambridge University Press.

——(1987) *Elementi di politica*. Bologna: il Mulino.

——(1994) "Neither Presidentialism nor Parliamentarism." In J. J. Linz and A. Valenzuela (eds), *The Failure of Presidential Democracy*, 106–18. Baltimore: Johns Hopkins University Press.

Schick, A. (1976) "Congress and the Details of Administration." *Public Administration Review* 36: 516–28.

Scott, R. (1987) "The Adolescence of Institutional Theory." *Administrative Studies Quarterly* 32.4: 493–511.

——(2001) *Institutions and Organizations*. 2nd edn; Thousand Oaks, CA: Sage Publications.

Shepsle, Kenneth (1989) "Studying Institutions: Some Lessons from Rational Choice Approach." *Journal of Theoretical Politics* 1: 131–47.

——(2006) "Rational Choice Institutionalism." In R. A. W. Rhodes, S. Binder and B. Rockman (eds), *Political Institutions*, 23–37. Oxford: Oxford University Press.

Skocpol, T. (2003) "Doubly Engaged Social Science." In James Mahoney and Ira Katznelson (eds), 407–28. *Comparative Historical Analysis in Social Sciences*. New York: Cambridge University Press.

Solomon Star (2008a) "More MPs Help Themselves with Forestry Money." 15 October.

——(2008b) "Ghiro: Blame Ministry of Finance." 15 October.

——(2008c) "Now Is Time to End the Abuse." 8 November.

Stapenhurst, F. (2011) "Legislative Oversight and Curbing Corruption: Presidentialism and Parliamentarianism Revised." PhD dissertation, Australian National University, Canberra.

Stapenhurst, F., and R. Pelizzo (2002) "A Bigger Role for Legislatures in Poverty Reduction." *Finance and Development. A Quarterly Publication of the International Monetary Fund* 39.4: 46–48.

Stapenhurst, R. (2011) "Presidentialism and Parliamentarianism Revisited." Unpublished PhD thesis, Australian National University.

Stapenhurst, R., and R. Pelizzo (2008) "Parliamentary Oversight and Corruption." Paper presented at the American Political Science Association conference, Chicago.

Stapenhurst, R., N. Johnston and R. Pelizzo (eds) (2006) *The Role of Parliament in Curbing Corruption*. Washington, DC: World Bank Institute.

Stapenhurst, R., R. Pelizzo, D. Olson and L. von Trapp (eds) (2008) *Legislative Oversight and Budgeting: A World Perspective*. Washington, DC: World Bank.

Stapenhurst, F., V. Saghal, W. Woodley and R. Pelizzo (2005) "Scrutinizing Public Expenditures: Assessing the Performance of Public Accounts Committees in Comparative Perspective." Policy Research Working Paper 3613, Washington DC: World Bank.

Stapenhurst, R., and J. Titsworth (2001) "Features and Functions of Supreme Audit Institutions." *PremNotes* 59. Washington, DC: World Bank.

Streek, W., and K. Thelen (2005) "Introduction: Institutional Change in Advanced Political Economies." In W. Steek and K. Thelen (eds), *Beyond Continuity: Institutional Change in Advanced Political Economies*, 1–39. Oxford: Oxford University Press.

Strom, K., W. Miller and T. Bergman (2000) *Delegation and Accountability in Parliamentary Democracies*. Oxford: Oxford University Press.

Tanzi, V., and H. Davoodi (1997) "Corruption, Public Investment, and Growth." *IMF Working Paper*.

Thelen, K., and S. Steinmo (1992) "Historical Institutionalism." In S. Steinmo, K. Thelen and F. Longstreth, *Comparative Politics*, 1–31. Cambridge: Cambridge University Press.

Treisman, D. (2000) "The Causes of Corruption: a Cross National Study." *Journal of Public Economics* 76.3: 399–457.

USAID (2000) *Handbook on Legislative Strengthening*. http://www.usaid.gov/our_work/democracy_and_governance/publications/pdfs/pnacf632.pdf.

Wang, V. (2005) "The Accountability Function of Parliament in New Democracies; Tanzanian Perspectives." *Christer Michelsen Institute Working Paper 2*. Bergen, Norway.

——(2003) "Principles and Patterns in Financial Scrutiny: Public Accounts Committees in the Commonwealth." *Commonwealth and Comparative Politics* 41.3: 21–36.

——(2004) "Back from the Sidelines? Redefining the Contribution of Legislatures to the Budget Cycle." *World Bank Institute Working Paper*. Washington, DC: World Bank.

Wehner, Joachim (2005) "Legislative Arrangements for Financial Scrutinity." In Riccardo Pelizzo, Rick Stapenhurst and David Olson (eds), *The Role of Parliament in the Budget Process*, 1–15. World Bank Institute Working Paper-Series on Contemporary Issues in Parliamentary Development; Washington, DC.

Wei, S.-J., and D. Kaufmann (1998) "Does 'Grease Money' Speed Up the Wheels of Commerce?" *International Monetary Fund*. Washington, DC. http://www.imf.org/external/pubs/cat/longres.cfm?sk=3524.0.

Weiner, Myron (1987) "Empirical Democratic Theory and the Transition from Authoritarianism to Democracy." *PS* 20.4: 861–66.

Weingast, B., and M. Moran (1983) "Bureaucratic Discretion or Congressional Control: Regulatory Policymaking in the Federal Trade Organization." *Journal of Political Economy* 91: 765–800.

World Bank (1997) *World Development Report: The Art of the State*. Washington, DC.

——(2000) *Anti-Corruption in Transition*. Washington, DC.

Yamamoto, H. (2008) *Tools of Parliamentary Oversight: A Comparative Study of 88 National Parliaments*. Geneva: Inter-Parliamentary Union.

Zucker, L. G. (1983) "Organizations as Institutions." In S. B. Bacharach (ed.), *Research in the Sociology of Organizations*, 1–42. Greenwich, CT: JAI Press.

Index

Printed in the USA/Agawam, MA
June 2, 2014

590428.136